CAPE TOWN
ARCHITECTURE & DESIGN

daab

Niederländische Siedler erreichten 1652 das Kap und sprenkelten die ländliche Gegend mit weiß getünchten, strohgedeckten Bauernhäusern. Die Briten fielen 150 Jahre später ein; bewaffnet mit den kunstvoll verzierten, fast überladenen Bauweisen für die Mittelklasse und Reihenhäusern für die Armen. Der Hafen, 1860 erbaut von Prinz Alfred, brachte Designeinflüsse aus anderen kulturellen Zentren nach Kapstadt. Um 1900 säumten Geschäfte mit Schaufenstern die Adderley Street, und das Mutual Building - das größte Gebäude Afrikas - wurde 1940 fertig gestellt. Zu dieser Zeit erweiterte ein ausgedehnter Landgewinnungsplan das Hafengebiet, um Schnellstraßen und einen modernen Hafen zu beherbergen. Die architektonischen Aktivitäten gingen während der Apartheid-Ära zurück, optimistische Planer begannen jedoch 1990, an der Victoria & Alfred Waterfront zu arbeiten. Die Verwandlung des Hafens in eine Uferattraktion schuf einen Kernpunkt für zukünftige, internationale Besucher. Im modernen Kapstadt nach der Apartheid-Ära, betonen Verjüngungsprojekte die Restauration und Rehabilitation der Stadt. Viele Bürokomplexe wurden in luxuriöse Lofts umfunktioniert, und junge Berufstätige bevölkern allmählich wieder den Geschäftsbezirk. Das Stadtbild bleibt einzigartig und wird geprägt durch den majestätischen Tafelberg und die umliegenden zwei Ozeane. Ausländische Investoren, die vom angenehmen Klima und den spektakulären Aussichten angezogen werden, haben wunderschöne Häuser an der Atlantikküste in Auftrag gegeben. Der Ozean, der als Quelle für die Bauweise Kapstadts gilt, inspiriert weiterhin Planer, die dieses Erbe bei ihrer zukünftigen Wachstumsplanung sorgfältig bewahren müssen.

Dutch settlers landed at the Cape in 1652 and dotted the rural landscape with whitewashed thatch-roofed homesteads. The British invaded 150-years later, armed with Queen Victoria's ornate designs for the middle classes, and terraced houses for the poor. The harbour, constructed by Prince Alfred in 1860, brought design influences from other cultural centers. By 1900, shops with display windows lined Adderley Street, and Mutual Building, the tallest in Africa, was completed in 1940. At this time, a massive land reclamation scheme extended the foreshore to accommodate freeways and a modern port. Architectural activity declined during the apartheid era, but optimistic developers began work on the Victoria & Alfred Waterfront in 1990. Turning the harbour into a waterside attraction created a nucleus for future international visitors. In post-apartheid Cape Town, regeneration projects emphasize the restoration and rehabilitation of the city. Many office blocks have been converted to luxury loft apartments, and young professionals are gradually repopulating the CBD. The city's image remains uniquely defined by the majesty of Table Mountain and the surrounding two oceans. Foreign investors, attracted by the temperate climate and spectacular views, have commissioned magnificent homes on the Atlantic seaboard. The ocean, as the origin of Cape Town's architectural styles, continues to inspire developers who must carefully maintain this heritage while planning for future growth.

Los colonos holandeses llegaron en 1652 al cabo de Buena Esperanza y salpicaron el paisaje rural de haciendas con tejados de paja. Los británicos invadieron el lugar 150 años más tarde. Las clases medias impusieron sus diseños ornamentados estilo Reina Victoria y los más pobres se conformaron con viviendas adosadas. A través del puerto, obra del Príncipe Alfred en 1860, llegaron influencias artísticas procedentes de otros centros culturales. Allá por el año 1900, las tiendas con escaparates se alineaban ya en la calle Adderley. El edificio Mutual, el más alto de África, se terminó de construir en 1940. Fue en ese momento cuando se aplicó un ambicioso plan de reordenamiento urbano que amplió la línea de costa con el fin de acomodar autopistas y un puerto moderno. La actividad arquitectónica se redujo durante la etapa del apartheid. Sin embargo, hubo promotores inmobiliarios con visión de futuro que comenzaron a trabajar en los muelles de Victoria & Albert en 1990. El puerto, transformado en una atracción a la orilla del mar, se convirtió en el foco de atención para los futuros visitantes de todo el mundo. Tras el apartheid, los proyectos de regeneración de Ciudad del Cabo hicieron hincapié en restaurar y rehabilitar la ciudad. Muchos edificios de oficinas se convirtieron en lujosos apartamentos estilo loft. Los jóvenes profesionales están volviendo a ocupar paulatinamente el centro de negocios. La imagen de la ciudad sigue siendo única. La majestuosidad del monte Table y los dos océanos circundantes la definen. Los inversores extranjeros, atraídos por el clima templado y las espectaculares vistas, han encargado la edificación de impresionantes viviendas en el litoral atlántico. El océano, al igual que el origen de los estilos arquitectónicos de Ciudad del Cabo, siguen sirviendo de inspiración a los diseñadores, quienes han de saber conservar la herencia al tiempo que planifican el crecimiento futuro.

Les colons hollandais ont débarqué au cap en 1652 et doté le paysage rural de propriétés en toits de chaume, blanchies à la chaux. Les Anglais ont envahi 159 ans plus tard, armés de designs d'ornements de la Reine Victoria pour les classes moyennes et de maison en terrasses pour les pauvres. Le port construit par le Prince Alfred en 1860 a apporté les influences de design d'autres centres culturels. En 1900, des boutiques avec des affichages en devantures longeaient l'Adderley Street, et Mutual Building, le plus grand bâtiment en Afrique a été achevé en 1940. À cette époque un schéma de réclamation massive dans le pays a élargi la laisse de mer pour adapter les autoroutes et un port moderne. L'activité architecturale a décliné durant l'ère de l'apartheid, mais des créateurs optimistes ont commencé à travailler sur le Victoria & Alfred Waterfront en 1990. La modification du port, rendu attrayant en bordure de mer, a créé un nucléus pour les visiteurs internationaux. Dans la ville du Cap post-apartheid, les projets de renouvellement soulignent la restauration et la réhabilitation de la ville. De nombreux blocs de bureaux ont été convertis en appartements de luxe loft et les jeunes professionnels sont en train de repeupler progressivement la CBD. L'image de la ville reste définie uniquement par la majesté de la Montagne de la Table et les deux océans environnants. Les investisseurs étrangers attirés par le climat tempéré et les vues spectaculaires ont commissionné des habitations magnifiques au bord de l'Océan Atlantique. L'océan, en tant qu'origine des styles architecturaux de la ville du Cap, continue à inspirer les créateurs qui doivent conserver soigneusement ce patrimoine en planifiant la croissance future.

I coloni olandesi sono approdati al Cape nel 1652 e hanno introdotto nel paesaggio rurale le case coloniche imbiancate con i tetti coperti di paglia. I britannici hanno invaso il territorio 150 anni più tardi, armati di progetti raffinati della Regina Vittoria per le classi medie e di case terrazzate per i poveri. Il porto, costruito dal Principe Alfred nel 1860, ha portato delle influenze di design da altri centri culturali. Nel 1900 i negozi con le vetrine erano allineati in Adderley Street e il Mutual Building, il più alto edificio dell'Africa, è stato completato nel 1940. A quel tempo, un massiccio piano di risanamento del territorio ha ampliato il litorale per ospitare le autostrade e un moderno scalo. L'attività architettonica è andata in declino durante il periodo dell'apartheid, ma degli sviluppatori ottimistici hanno iniziato nel 1990 a costruire il Lungomare Victoria & Alfred. La trasformazione del porto in un'attrazione sul litorale ha creato un nucleo per visitatori internazionali futuri. Nella Cape Town post-apartheid i progetti di rigenerazione enfatizzano il restauro e la riabilitazione della città. Molti palazzi di uffici sono stati trasformati in lussuosi appartamenti loft e giovani professionisti stanno gradualmente ripopolando il CBD. L'immagine della città rimane definita in modo unico dalla maestosità del Table Mountain e dai due oceani circostanti. Investitori stranieri, attratti dal clima temperato e dal panorama spettacolare, hanno commissionato delle case magnifiche sulla costa atlantica. L'oceano, come l'origine degli stili architettonici di Cape Town, continua a ispirare i progettisti che devono mantenere questa eredità con cautela e al contempo progettare la crescita futura.

Albert&Partners, Architecture and Design
Higgovale Hideaway | 2004
Kloof Nek Road, Higgovale, Cape Town
Photos: David Southwood

Für die umfangreiche Neugestaltung dieses alten, an den Hängen des Tafelbergs gelegenen Bungalows, mussten die Planer den Kontext seiner Lage und der umgebenden Flora berücksichtigen. Der Garten wurde so gestaltet, dass eine Unterhaltungsterrasse für die neue, untere Räumlichkeit geschaffen werden konnte. Durch den geschickten Einsatz von Spiegeln auf der inneren Stützwand dieser Etage verschmilzt das Haus scheinbar mit seiner Umgebung.

When substantially remodeling this old bungalow on the slopes of Table Mountain, the designers had to consider the context of its location and surrounding flora. The garden was built up to create an entertainment terrace for the new lower ground accommodation. The clever use of mirror on the interior retaining wall of this level makes the house appear to blend entirely into its surroundings.

A la hora de remodelar este antiguo bungalow en la ladera del monte Table, los proyectistas debieron tener en cuenta su ubicación y la flora del entorno. El diseño del jardín incluía una terraza de esparcimiento para el nuevo apartamento de la planta inferior. Con el uso ingenioso de los espejos en el muro de contención interior de este nivel se consigue una integración completa de la vivienda en su entorno.

En remodelant substantiellement ce vieux bungalow sur les collines de la Montagne de la Table, les designers ont dû considérer le contexte de son emplacement et la flore environnante. Le jardin a été aménagé pour créer une terrasse de loisirs au nouveau rez-de-chaussée de l'habitation. L'utilisation intelligente d'un miroir sur le mur de cet étage retenant l'intérieur donne l'impression que la maison se confond avec l'environnement.

Nel rimodellare essenzialmente questo vecchio bungalow sui versanti di Table Mountain i progettisti hanno dovuto considerare il contesto del luogo e della flora circostante. Il giardino è stato costruito per creare una terrazza di intrattenimento per il nuovo alloggio del piano inferiore. L'utilizzo intelligente di specchi sulla parete conservatrice di questo piano fa apparire la casa come se si mescolasse interamente ai suoi dintorni.

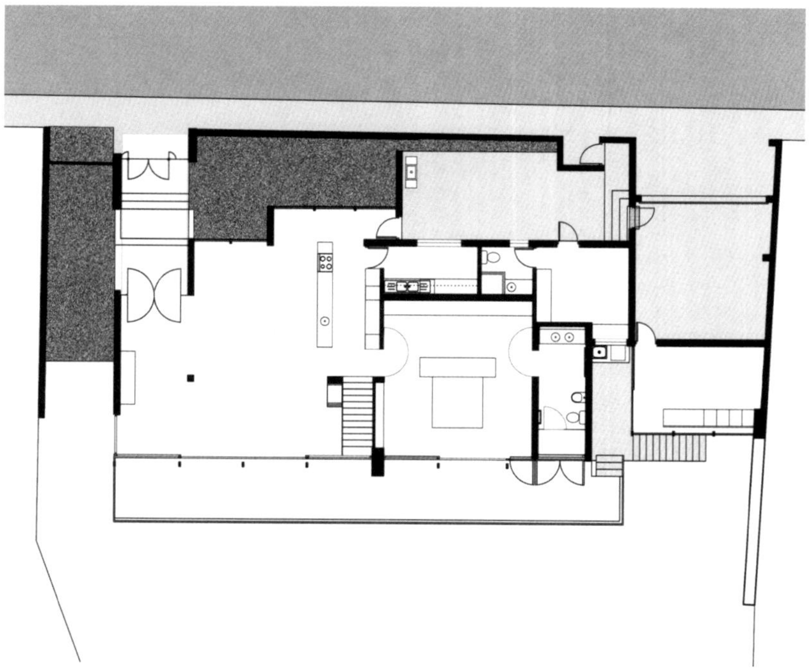

Albert&Partners, Architecture and Design
Organic House | 2007
Bishops Court, Cape Town
Photos: Renderings Don Albert/soundspacedesign, David Southwood

Die geschwungene, futuristische Architektur dieses in Bishop's Court gelegenen Hauses kontrastiert erheblich mit seiner konservativen Umgebung. Zwei Bäder, die jeweils zu den Hauptschlafzimmern gehören, bilden den baulichen Kern des Gebäudes. Eine Brücke, die diese zwei Bereiche miteinander verbindet, ist mit fließenden Blenden aus Balauholz verkleidet. Dieser Bereich ist durch ein barockes Terrazzo-Treppenhaus zu erreichen, das sich über einer von hinten beleuchteten Onyx-Bar erhebt. Der Innenbereich wurde mit elfenbeinfarbigem Quarzit sowie Buchen- und Kampferbaumholz veredelt, um ein warmes, softes Familienheim zu kreieren.

The curved, futuristic architecture of this Bishop's Court house contrasts strongly with its conservative surroundings. Two bathrooms, each servicing main bedroom areas, form the structural cores of the building. A bridge connecting the two sections is clad in flowing screens of Balau timber. This level is accessed by a baroque terrazzo staircase, rising above a backlit onyx bar. Interior finishes in ivory quartzite, beech and camphor create a warm, soft, family home.

La arquitectura sinuosa y futurista de la casa Bishop's Court contrasta con un entorno más conservador. Dos baños, destinados a los dormitorios, conforman los núcleos estructurales de la construcción. Un puente recubierto con balau comunica las dos secciones. A este se accede por una escalera barroca de terrazo, que conduce a un bar iluminado en ónice. El interior es de marfil, haya y resina de alcanfor, creando una casa cálida y acogedora.

L'architecture courbée et futuriste de cette demeure des évêques contraste fortement avec les environnements conservateurs. Deux salles de bains, reliée chacune à la chambre principale, créent les noyaux structurels du bâtiment. Un pont reliant les deux sections est revêtu de bois de Balau. Cet étage est accessible par un escalier terrasse baroque, surplombant un bar en onyx, éclairé par l'arrière.

L'architettura curvata e futuristica di questo vicariato contrasta fortemente con i suoi dintorni conservativi. Due camere da letto, ognuna a servizio delle zone da letto principali, formano il cuore strutturale dell'edificio. Un ponte che collega i due settori è rivestito da schermi scorrevoli di legno Balau. Ci si accede da una scala a terrazzo barocca che si eleva sopra una sbarra retroilluminata in onice. Le rifiniture interne in avorio quarzite, faggio e canfora creano una casa calda, morbida e familiare.

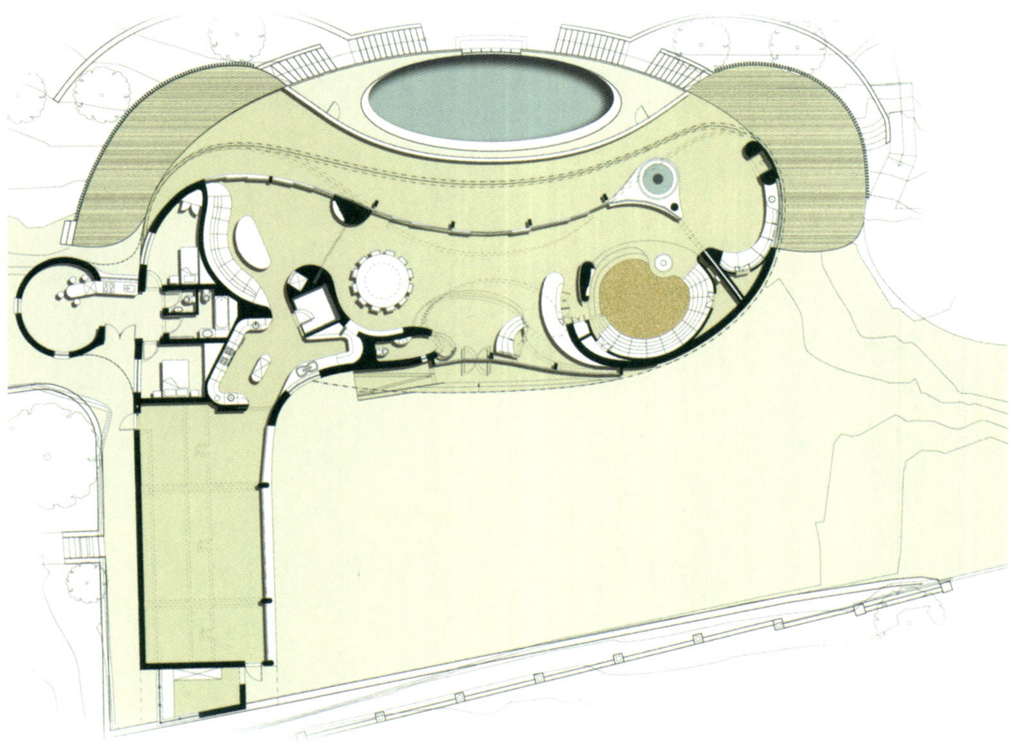

Albert&Partners, Architecture and Design
Soundspace1 | 2006
Loop Street, City Bowl, Cape Town
Photos: Angie Lazaro

Die Anpassung dieses 1950 erbauten Bürokomplexes kombiniert ein Heim mit einem Arbeitsstudio zu einem flexiblen Arrangement innerhalb einer zweckmäßigen Stadtlage. Dramatische, weiße Vorhänge trennen die Wohn- und Bürobereiche voneinander, und Türen mit schwarzen Lamellenjalousien lassen eine dynamische Anpassung an das Interieur zu. Hier herrscht ein spannender Kontrast zwischen der hellen, luftigen Atmosphäre des Designstudios gegenüber den farbenfrohen, poppigen Ausstattungen der Wohnbereiche.

The adaptation of this 1950s office block combines a home and work studio into one flexible arrangement within a convenient city location. Dramatic white curtains divide the residential and office spaces, and black roller-shutter doors allow dynamic adjustment of the interior. There is exciting contrast between the light, airy atmosphere of the design studio versus the colorful pop furnishings in the living areas.

La adaptación de este bloque de oficinas de los años 50 combina vivienda y trabajo en un alojamiento flexible situado en una zona privilegiada de la ciudad. Unas llamativas cortinas blancas dividen las zonas de vivienda y trabajo y unas puertas plegables en negro permiten reconfigurar el interior de manera dinámica. El contraste entre la atmósfera liviana del estudio de diseño y el colorido pop del mobiliario de la vivienda es muy atractivo.

L'adaptation de ce bloc de bureaux des années cinquante combine une maison d'habitation et un atelier de travail avec des possibilités d'aménagement flexible à l'intérieur de cette maison de charme. Des rideaux blancs spectaculaires divisent les espaces résidentiels et les espaces de bureaux, et des portes à volets roulants permettent l'ajustement dynamique de l'intérieur. Il y a un contraste excitant entre l'atmosphère, légère et aérée de l'atelier contre l'ameublement pop multicolore dans les aires de vie.

L'adattamento di questo palazzo di uffici degli anni '50 combina una casa e uno studio da lavoro in un singolo allestimento flessibile all'interno di un luogo cittadino. Delle sensazionali tende bianche dividono le aree residenziali da quelle di lavoro e delle porte nere di persiane avvolgibili consentono un adeguamento dinamico dell'interno. Sussiste un contrasto eccitante tra la luce, l'atmosfera aerea dello studio di design e l'arredamento pop colorato delle zone abitative.

Arthur Quinton Darryl Croome Architects
House Quinton I 2003
Avenue Disandt, Fresnaye, Cape Town
Photos: Andrea Getuli

Unbehandelte, natürliche Materialien sind der Garant für die kühne Aussage in diesem trendigen, südafrikanischen Heim, das sich von gestrichenen Wänden und konventioneller Möblierung klar distanziert. Durch die Verwendung von Shutters und hohen Decken kann auf Aircondition in diesem warmen Klima verzichtet werden. Eine geschickte Anordnung von großzügigen Räumen und tiefen Überhängen erlauben es dem Licht, der Luft und der Aussicht in jeden Teil des Hauses einzutreten.

Raw, natural materials make a bold statement in this contemporary South African home that moves away from painted walls and conventional finishes. The use of shutters and high ceilings avoids the need for air conditioning in this warm climate. A clever arrangement of double-volume spaces and deep overhangs allows light, air and views to enter every part of the house.

Los materiales naturales y sin tratar son toda una declaración de intenciones de esta moderna vivienda que se aleja de las paredes pintadas y de los acabados convencionales. Los postigos y los techos altos permiten renunciar al aire acondicionado. Una disposición inteligente de volúmenes dobles y grandes aleros aportan luz, aire y panorámicas a cada rincón de la casa.

Les matériaux naturels sont des composants audacieux dans cette habitation sud africaine contemporaine qui s'écarte des murs peints et des finitions conventionnelles. L'utilisation de volets et de hauts plafonds évitent le besoin en air conditionné dans ce climat chaud. La combinaison intelligente de doubles espaces et de rebords permet la pénétration de la lumière et offre des vues panoramiques dans chaque partie de l'habitation.

Materiali grezzi e naturali mettono un punto coraggioso in questa casa contemporanea del Sud Africa, che si allontana della pareti dipinte e da rifiniture convenzionali. L'utilizzo di persiane e di alti soffitti evitano la necessità di un'aria condizionata con questo clima caldo. Un arrangiamento intelligente di spazi doppi e profonde sporgenze permettono alla luce, all'aria e al panorama di entrare in ogni parte della casa.

Arthur Quinton Darryl Croome Architects
House Stefanutti | 2006
Top Road, Fresnaye, Cape Town
Photos: The Graphic Ballroom

Man gelangt zu diesem anspruchsvollen, modernen Heim über eine aus Balau-Holz gefertigte Brücke, die zur Eingangstür aus Stahl und Mahagoni führt. Um vom angenehmen Klima Kapstadts zu profitieren, ermöglicht eine überdachte Terrasse das Dinieren im Freien sowie spektakuläre Ausblicke auf den Atlantischen Ozean jenseits eines Pools mit Überlaufrinnensystem. Eine mit Steinen verkleidete Wand kontrastiert mit dem schwebenden Treppenhaus, das zu vier Schlafzimmern und ihren mit Bad und WC ausgestatteten Bädern führt. Das bepflanzte Atrium schafft natürliches Licht für die unteren Ebenen.

Entry to this sophisticated, modern home is via a Balau wood bridge to the stainless steel and mahogany door. Taking advantage of Cape Town's temperate climate, an enclosed terrace allows al fresco dining and spectacular views of the Atlantic Ocean beyond a rimflow pool. A rock clad wall contrasts with the floating staircase that leads to four bedrooms and their en suit bathrooms. The planted atrium provides natural light for the lower levels.

A esta sofisticada casa se entra por un puente de madera de balau y atravesando un puerta de acero inoxidable y caoba. Aprovechando el clima tan benigno de la ciudad, la terraza permite cenar al aire libre y ofrece vistas espectaculares sobre el Atlántico por encima de una piscina de rebosadero. Una pared revestida de roca contrasta con la escalera flotante que lleva a los cuatro dormitorios. El atrio surte de luz natural a los niveles inferiores.

L'entrée de cette habitation moderne et sophistiquée est accessible par un pont en bois de Balau jusqu'à la porte en acier inoxydable et en mahagoni. Bénéficiant du climat tempéré de la ville du Cap, une terrasse clôturée permet de dîner au frais et de contempler des panoramas spectaculaires sur l'Océan Atlantique au-delà de la piscine à débordement. Un mur de parement en pierre contraste avec la cage d'escaliers flottante qui mène aux chambres et aux salles de bains en suites. L'atrium construit fournit une lumière naturelle aux étages inférieurs.

L'entrata in questa casa sofisticata e moderna avviene tramite un ponte di legno Balau verso la porta di acciaio inossidabile e di mogano. Una terrazza chiusa, che prende vantaggio dal clima temperato di Cape Town, consente di cenare all'aperto e di godere di una vista spettacolare dell'Oceano Atlantico al di là della piscina a filo d'acqua. Una parete rivestita di roccia contrasta con la scalinata fluttuante che porta a quattro camere da letto e ai loro bagni en suit. L'atrio con piante fornisce la luce naturale per i livelli inferiori.

Arthur Quinton Darryl Croome Architects
House Williams | 2006
Head Road, Fresnaye, Cape Town
Photos: Anthony Allen, Andrea Getuli

Innen- und Außenbereich gehen nahtlos ineinander über, wodurch das natürliche Licht optimal verstärkt wird und atemberaubende Aussichten aus diesem einzigartigen Heim heraus ermöglicht werden. Die sich im Freien befindliche Poolterasse bildet den Schwerpunkt für den Lebensraum, der perfekt auf Entertaining zugeschnitten wurde. Separate Bereiche zum Leben, Essen sowie Schlafräume und Gästeunterkünfte werden durch großzügige Räume miteinander verbunden, und eine Brücke markiert den Eingang zur Mastersuite. Das Nachmittagssonnenlicht wird durch Shutters aus Aluminium und Holz in Schach gehalten.

A seamless flow from indoors to outdoors maximises the natural light and breathtaking views from this unique home. The al fresco pool terrace provides a focal point for the living space which is perfectly suited to entertaining. Separate areas for living, dining, bedrooms and guest accommodation are connected by double-volume spaces, and a bridge defines entry to the master suite. Afternoon sunlight is controlled by aluminium and wood shutters.

Un flujo continuo del interior al exterior amplifica la luz natural y las impresionantes vistas de esta casa. La terraza al aire libre con piscina sirve de núcleo del área de ocio ideada para el esparcimiento. Sala de estar, comedor, dormitorios y cuarto de invitados se comunican por espacios de doble volumen. Un puente sirve de entrada a la habitación principal. La luz del atardecer se controla con postigos de aluminio y madera.

Le flux intégré de l'intérieur à l'extérieur maximise la lumière naturelle et les vues panoramiques à vous couper le souffle de cette habitation unique. La terrasse de la piscine toute fraîche représente le point central de l'espace d'habitation, parfaitement adaptée aux loisirs. L'aire séparée de la salle à manger, des chambres et des chambres d'hôtes sont reliées par de doubles espaces et un pont définit l'entrée de la suite de maître. La lumière de l'après-midi est contrôlée par des volets en aluminium et en bois.

Un flusso continuo dall'interno all'esterno massimizza la luce naturale e la vista mozzafiato di questa casa unica. La terrazza della piscina all'aperto fornisce il punto focale dell'area abitativa che è perfettamente adatta all'intrattenimento. Le distinte aree da soggiorno, da pranzo, da letto e per l'ospitalità sono collegate tramite spazi doppi. Un ponte definisce l'entrata alla suite principale. La luce del sole pomeridiano è controllata grazie a persiane di alluminio e di legno.

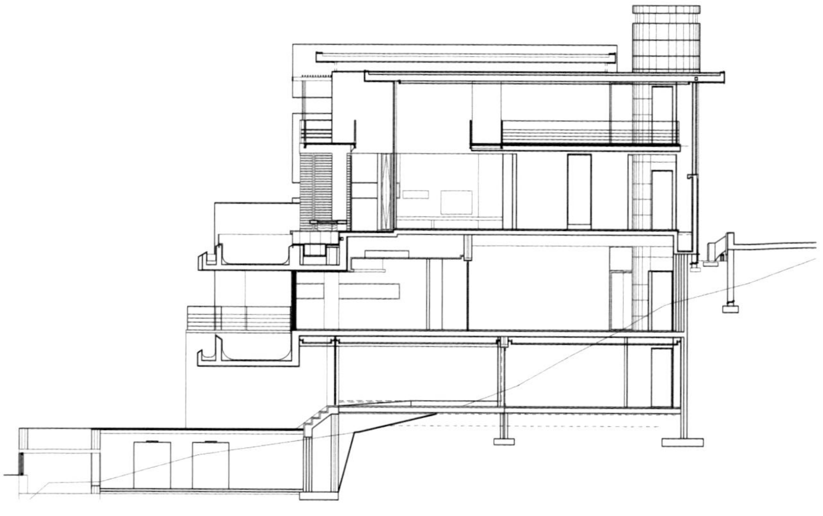

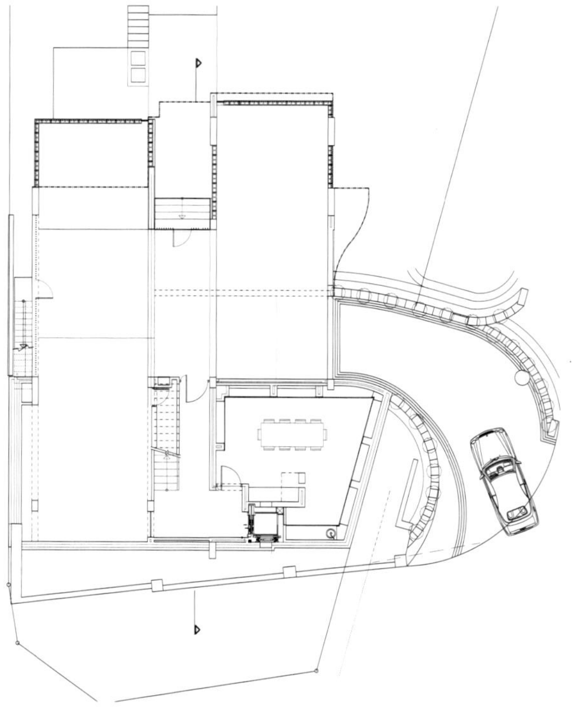

THE EARTH FROM THE AIR

Arthur Quinton Darryl Croome Architects
Metropolis | 2006
Chiappini Street, Greenpoint, Cape Town
Photos: Anthony Allen

Der Hauptsitz dieses Architekten betont durch seine kühnen, modernen Linien und sein Industriefinish die verwendeten Rohmaterialien. Die, mit roten Vorsatzziegeln und aus der Umgebung stammenden Steinen verkleidete Betonkonstruktion mit doppelter Wandstärke, reflektiert die umliegenden Hafengebäude. In den offenen Studios und spannenden Loftbereichen kontrastieren auserwählte, erlesene Einrichtungen mit den natürlichen, rauen Strukturen des Gebäudes.

As the head office of this architect, its bold, modern lines and industrial finish highlight the raw materials of their trade. The concrete double volume structure, clad in red face brick and local stone, reflects the surrounding harbor buildings. In its open-plan studios and exciting loft spaces, selected fine fittings contrast with the natural, rough textures of the building.

Al tratarse de las oficinas de este arquitecto, las líneas modernas y atrevidas y el acabado industrial resaltan el uso de materiales sin tratar propios del sector. La doble estructura de hormigón revestido con ladrillo rojo y piedra autóctona refleja los edificios del puerto. Los espacios diáfanos y el selecto mobiliario contrastan con las texturas naturales y rugosas del edificio.

Siège social de cet architecte : ses lignes audacieuses et modernes, et sa finition industrielle illustrent les matériaux bruts utilisés. La double structure en béton, le parement en brique de ravalement rouge et en pierre locale, redonnent l'image des bâtiments de port environnants. Dans ses studios ouverts et ses espaces loft excitants, les équipements finement sélectionnés contrastent avec les textures naturelles, brutes du bâtiment.

In quanto sede principale di questo architetto, le sue linee audaci e moderne, oltre alla rifinitura industriale sottolineano i materiali grezzi dell'attività. La struttura doppia di cemento, rivestita con mattoni a vista rossi e pietra locale, riflette gli edifici circostanti del porto. Nei suoi studi a pianta aperta e negli spazi eccitanti dei loft, gli impianti finemente selezionati contrastano con i tessuti naturali e grezzi dell'edificio.

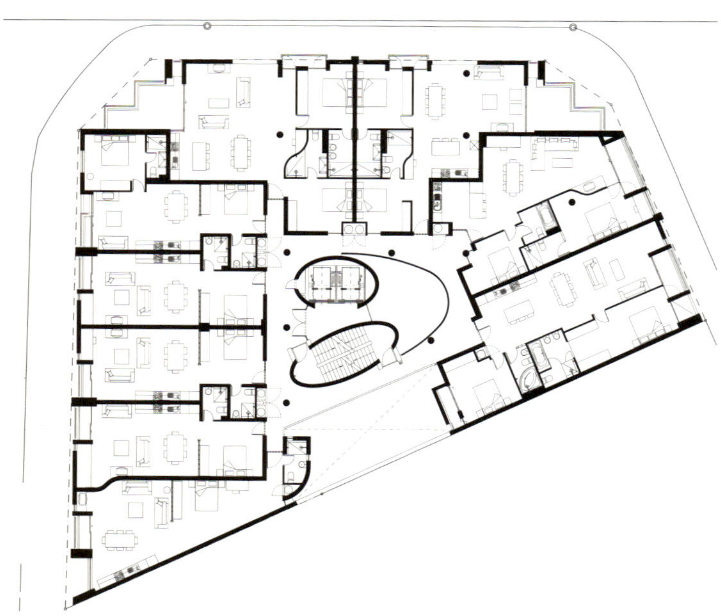

ON SHOW
WEEKDAYS
SUNDAYS

dhk

Icon | 2007

Loop, Hans Strijdom & Long Streets, City Bowl, Cape Town

Photos: Derick Henstra

Diese Planung vereint einzelhandelsspezifische, unternehmerische und wohnspezifische Funktionen. Eine Glasfassade und ein Dach über der Laufzone lassen Tageslicht herein, wodurch ein Straßeneinkaufserlebnis simuliert wird. Stahl- und Holzbrücken verbinden den Bürokomplex und die mit Sandstein gepflasterten Parkebenen, während ein Pooldeck die Verkaufsebenen von den Wohnebenen trennt. Der luxuriöse Appartementturm umschließt ein offenes Atrium, wodurch eine natürliche Belüftung und Ausblicke auf die Umgebung ermöglicht werden.

This development combines retail, corporate and residential functions. A glass facade and roof over the pedestrian walkway permits daylight and simulates a street shopping experience. Steel and timber bridges link the office block and sandstone clad parking levels, while a pool deck separates the retail and residential levels. The luxury apartment tower curves around an open atrium, allowing natural ventilation and surrounding views.

Este edificio combina pequeño comercio, oficinas y residencia. La fachada y el techado de cristal que cubre la acera dejan pasar la luz. Da la sensación de ir de compras por la calle. Unos puentes de acero y madera comunican el bloque de oficinas con el aparcamiento revestido de arenisca. Los comercios y la zona residencial están unidos por la planta con la piscina. La torre de viviendas gira en torno a un atrio que ofrece ventilación y vistas panorámicas.

Ce lotissement combine les fonctions de détail, d'association et de résidence. Une façade de verre et un toit au-dessus de l'allée piétonne permet la pénétration de la lumière du jour et stimule l'expérience du shopping de rue. Les ponts en acier et en bois relient le bloc de bureaux et les étages de parking avec des parements en grès, tandis que la plage de piscine sépare l'aire de commerce de détail et les étages résidentiels. La tour d'appartements de luxe se courbe, permettant la ventilation naturelle et des vues sur les alentours.

Questo sviluppo combina la funzione di vendita al dettaglio con quella aziendale e quella residenziale. Una facciata e un tetto di vetro sopra al camminatoio per le persone consente il passaggio della luce del giorno e simula la sensazione dello shopping per strada. Dei ponti di acciaio e legno uniscono il palazzo di uffici e i livelli del parcheggio rivestiti di arenaria, mentre la pavimentazione della piscina separa il livello della vendita al dettaglio dal livello residenziale. La lussuosa torre di appartamenti gira intorno ad un atrio aperto, rendendo possibile una ventilazione naturale e una vista dei dintorni.

icon

TO LET
OFFICE AND RETAIL SPACE

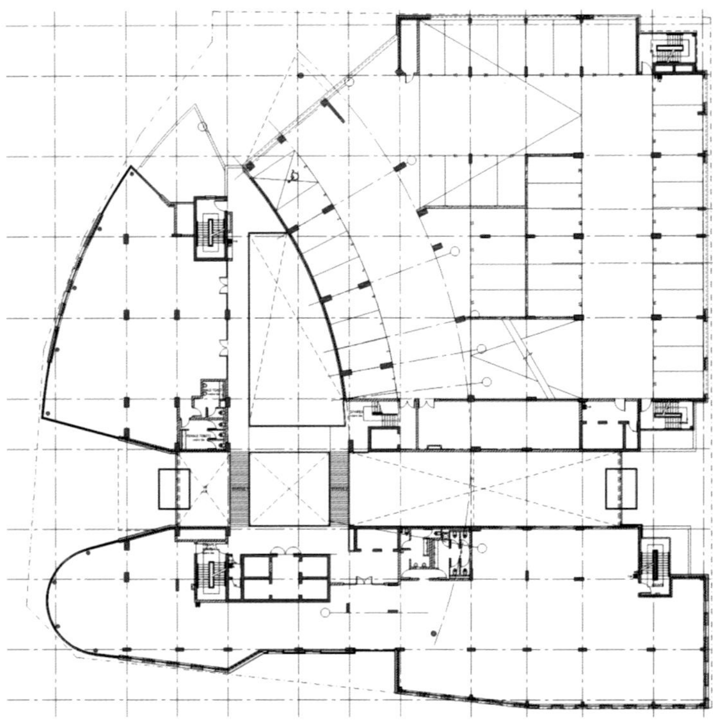

icon

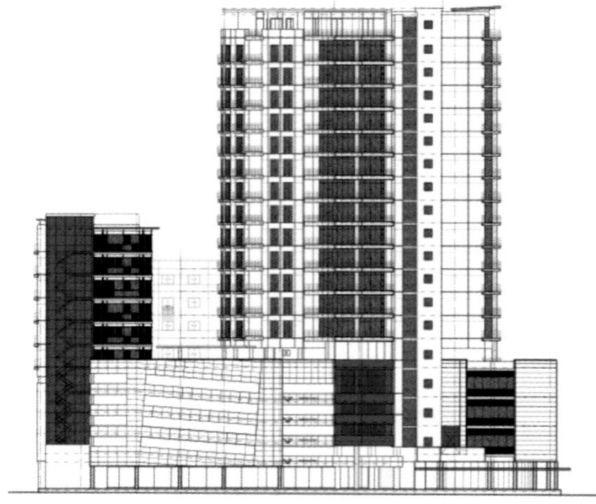

dhk
Mandela Rhodes Place | 2007
St George's Mall & Wale Street, City Bowl, Cape Town
Photos: Derick Henstra

Viele bestehende Gebäude auf diesem Gelände wurden erhalten, um der historischen Bedeutung den gebührenden Respekt zu zollen. Die oberen Etagen wurden in Appartements mit Ausblick auf die Stadt und das Gebirge umfunktioniert, während die unteren Stockwerke offen gestaltet wurden, um die Sichtbarkeit und den Verkaufsraum zu vergrößern. Die Tiefgarage wurde hinter einer erhaltenen Fassade gebaut, und direkt darüber befindet sich ein zentraler, verglaster Appartementturm. Bestehende Untergeschosse und Gewölbe beherbergen Kellerräume für eine großzügige städtische Weinkellerei.

Many existing buildings on this site were retained to respect their historic significance. Upper floors were converted to apartments with views of the city and mountain, while lower levels were opened to increase visibility and retail space. The parking garage was constructed behind a preserved facade, and a central glazed apartment tower built above that. Existing basements and vaults house fermentation cellars for a double volume urban winery.

Muchos de los edificios de esta zona se conservaron por su valor histórico. Las plantas superiores se convirtieron en viviendas con vistas a la ciudad y a la montaña, Los pisos inferiores se abrieron para aumentar la visibilidad y crear comercios. Se construyó un garaje tras la fachada, que se mantuvo, y sobre este una torre acristalada. Los sótanos y bóvedas existentes sirven hoy de bodegas urbanas de fermentación con el doble de capacidad.

De nombreux bâtiments existants sur ce site ont été retenus pour respecter leur signification historique. Les étages supérieurs ont été convertis en appartements avec des vues sur la ville et la montagne tandis que les étages inférieurs ont été ouverts pour augmenter la visibilité et l'espace de détail. Le garage parking a été construit derrière une façade préservée et une tour d'appartements centrale vernissée, construite au-dessus. Les fondations existantes et les voûtes abritent les celliers de fermentation doublant le volume de vignobles urbains.

Molti edifici esistenti in quest'area sono stati mantenuti per rispettare il loro significato storico. I piani superiori sono stati trasformati in appartamenti con vista sulla città e sulle montagne, mentre i piani inferiori sono stati aperti per aumentare la visibilità e gli spazi per la vendita al dettaglio. Il parcheggio coperto è stato costruito dietro a una facciata preservata e una torre di appartamenti, invetriata e centrale, costruita sopra di esso. Le fondamenta esistenti e i sotterranei ospitano le cantine di fermentazione per una doppia azienda vinicola urbana.

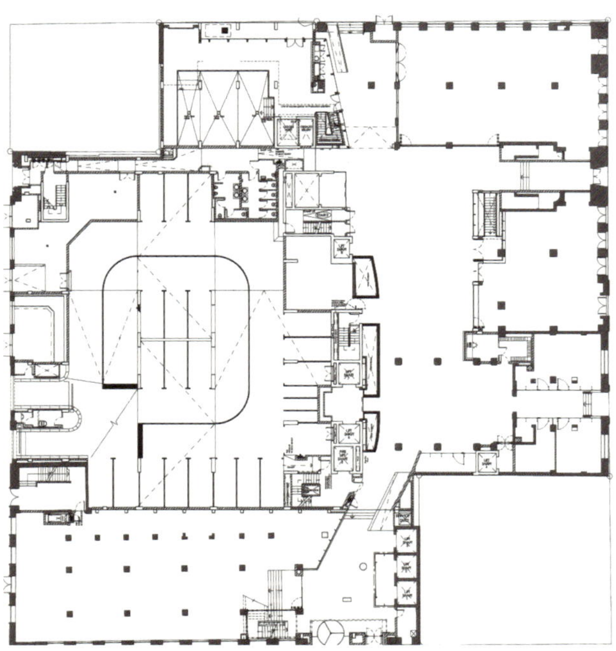

Gabriel Fagan Architects
Wolfson Pavilion | 2005
University of Cape Town, Observatory, Cape Town
Photos: Gavin Dingle

Ein markanter, zylindrischer Turm verbindet die beiden Gebäude, die das Institut für Infektionskrankheiten und Molekularmedizin bilden. Vom Boden bis zur Decke reichendes Glas spiegelt respektvoll die neo-klassischen Fassaden und gibt einen wunderschönen Blick auf den Devil's Peak frei, während bewegliche, vertikale Jalousien das gleißende Nachmittagssonnenlicht filtern. Großzügige Treppenpodeste und möblierte Rezeptionsbereiche ermutigen zur Interaktion zwischen den Fachabteilungen.

A distinctive cylindrical tower links the two buildings that form The Institute of Infectious Disease and Molecular Medicine. Its floor to ceiling glass respectfully reflects their neo-classical facades and reveals a magnificent view of Devil's Peak, while moveable vertical louvres filter the harsh afternoon sunlight. Generous stair landings and furnished reception areas encourage interaction between departments.

Esta original torre cilíndrica comunica los dos edificios del Instituto de Enfermedades Infecciosas y Medicina Molecular. El cristal, desde el suelo al tejado, refleja las fachadas neoclásicas y ofrece una panorámica magnífica de Devil's Peak. Las tablillas a modo de persianas venecianas en vertical filtran la molesta luz de la tarde. Los amplios descansillos y el mobiliario de la recepción fomentan la interacción entre los diferentes departamentos.

Une tour cylindrique distinctive relie les deux bâtiments qui créent l'institut de maladies infectieuses et de médecine moléculaire ; Son verre, du plancher jusqu'au plafond, renvoient respectueusement l'image des façades néoclassiques et révèlent une vue magnifique sur le Pic du Diable, tandis que les volets d'aération filtrent la lumière du soleil d'un après-midi chaud. Les vastes cages d'escalier et les aires de réception aménagées encouragent l'interaction entre les départements.

Una caratteristica torre cilindrica collega i due edifici che formano l'Istituto per Malattie Infettive e Medicina Molecolare. La vetrata cielo-terra riflette in modo rispettoso le loro facciate neo-classiche e rivela una vista magnifica del Devil's Peak, mentre delle persiane movibili verticalmente filtrano la penetrante luce del sole pomeridiano. Degli atri di scala generosi e delle zone reception arredate incoraggiano l'interazione tra i reparti.

IOUS DISEASE
MEDICINE
OF INFECTIOUS DISEASE AN MOLECULAR

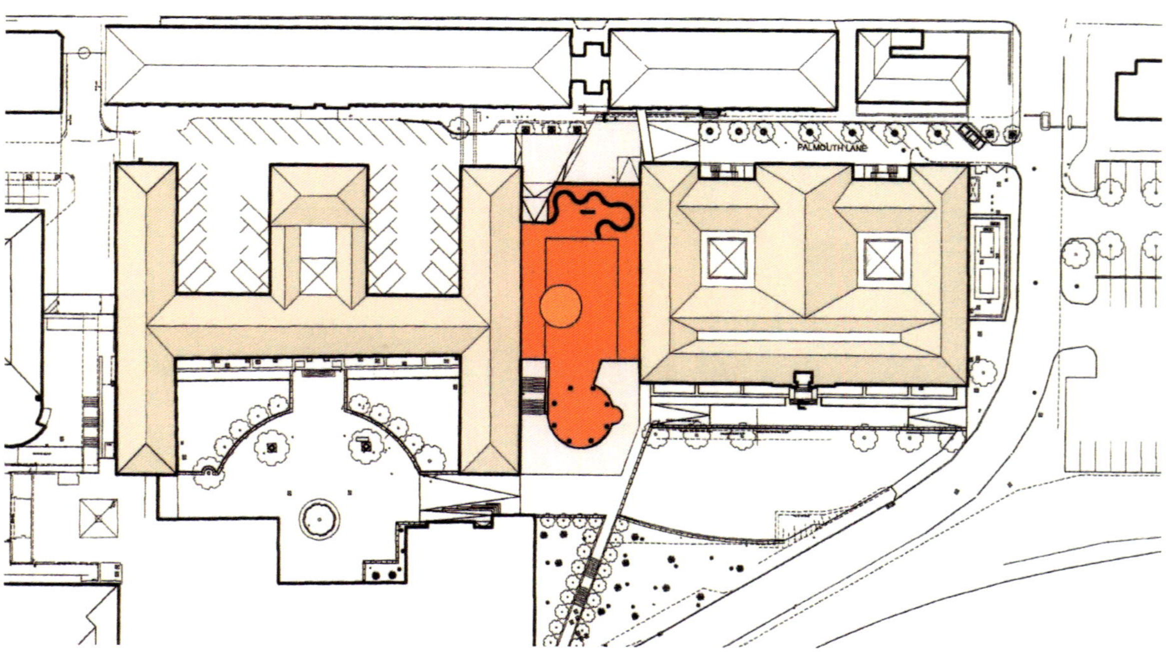
PALMOUTH LANE

WERNHER AND BEIT MEDICAL LABORATORIES.
UNIVERSITY OF CAPE TOWN.

GAPP
Westin Grand Hotel | 2003
Convention Square, Lower Long Street, Foreshore, Cape Town
Photos: Starwood Archive

Diese luxeröse Planung dehnt die Straßenführung bis hin zum vorgelagerten Uferland aus und befindet sich über dem neuen Kanal, der den Geschäftsbezirk mit dem historischen Hafenviertel, der Victoria & Alfred Waterfront, verbindet. Durchgängige Glaswände spiegeln den Himmel und das Stadtbild, und sein 19-geschossiger Turm bietet unübertroffene Ausblicke auf den Ozean und den Tafelberg. Durch die Integration in die Konstruktion des internationalen Kongresszentrums, ergänzen sich die beiden Komplexe, während sie jedoch unabhängig voneinander fungieren.

This luxurious development extends the city grid onto the Foreshore and is situated on the new canal linking the CBD to the historic Victoria & Alfred Waterfront. Continuous glass walls reflect the sky and cityscape, and its 19-storey tower provides unsurpassed views of the ocean and Table Mountain. Integrated into the construction of the International Convention Centre, the two complexes compliment each other while operating independently.

Esta lujosa edificación extiende el entramado urbano a la línea de playa. Se encuentra junto al nuevo canal que une el centro de negocios con los muelles de Victoria & Alfred. Las paredes de cristal reflejan el cielo y la silueta de la ciudad. Con sus 19 plantas, esta torre ofrece unas vistas inigualables del océano y de la montaña Table. Se integra en el Centro Internacional de Convenciones, aunque ambos complejos operan de forma independiente.

Ce lotissement luxueux prolonge la grille de ville jusqu'à la laisse de mer. Il est situé sur le nouveau canal, reliant la CBD au Victoria & Alfred Waterfront historique. Des murs en verre sans fin redonnent l'image du ciel et du paysage urbain, et la tour à dix-neuf étages offre des vues imprenables sur l'océan et la Montagne de la Table. Intégrés dans la construction du Centre de convention internationale, les deux complexes se complètent l'un et l'autre, tout en opérant indépendamment.

Questo lussuoso sviluppo estende la griglia della città fino alla spiaggia ed è posto sul nuovo canale, in modo da collegare il CBD al litorale storico Victoria & Alfred. Le pareti a vetro riflettono il cielo e il paesaggio della città e la sua torre di 19 piani fornisce una vista insuperabile dell'oceano e della Table Mountain. Integrati nella costruzione dell'International Convention Centre, i due complessi si completano a vicenda, mentre operano indipendentemente.

THE
TOWERS
CLUB

Louis B's

gmp - von Gerkan, Marg und Partner - Architects
Greenpoint Stadium | due 2009
Greenpoint, Cape Town
Photos/Visualisation: gmp - von Gerkan, Marg und Partner - Architects/MACINA, gmp Architects

Dieses zum Austragen von Fußballspielen geplante Stadium bietet Sitze für circa 68.000 Zuschauer, die sich über drei Ränge erstrecken. Die Außenhaut aus hellem Glasfasergewebe soll die Farben des Tageslichts reflektieren und ein Gefühl von Tiefe und Lebhaftigkeit hervorrufen. Die Formen des Interieurs wurden so gewählt, dass sie die Aufmerksamkeit auf das Spielfeld lenken, wodurch eine intensive und spannende Atmosphäre entsteht. Das Stadium ist dazu bestimmt, eines der Wahrzeichen der Stadt zu werden.

Designed to accommodate football games, the stadium seats approximately 68,000 spectators, divided over three tiers. The exterior shell of light glass-fiber tissue is intended to reflect the color of existing daylight and create a sense of depth and animation. Interior shapes are designed to focus all attention on the playing field, ensuring an intense and exciting atmosphere. The stadium is destined to become one of the city's landmarks.

Diseñado para albergar partidos de fútbol, este estadio tiene un aforo para 68.000 espectadores dividido en tres gradas. La cubierta, de fibra de carbono muy ligera, tiene por objeto reflejar la luz diurna y generar así la sensación de profundidad y movimiento. Las formas interiores se han diseñado para centrar la atención en la cancha, garantizando un ambiente intenso y apasionante. Está destinado a convertirse en uno de los símbolos de la ciudad.

Conçu pour accueillir les matchs de football, le stade a de la place pour 68 000 spectateurs environ, divisé sur trois tiers. La coquille extérieure en tissu de fibre de verre doit réfléchir la couleur de la lumière du jour existante, créant une sensation de profondeur et d'animation. Les formes intérieures sont conçues pour concentrer toute l'attention sur le terrain de jeu, garantissant une atmosphère intense et excitante. Le stade est destiné à devenir l'une des images de marque de la ville.

Progettato per ospitare le partite di football, lo stadio dà posto a circa 68.000 spettatori, suddivisi in tre tribune. Il guscio esterno di leggero tessuto di fibra vitrea ha lo scopo di riflettere il colore della luce del giorno e creare un senso di profondità e animazione. Le forme interne sono progettate per focalizzare tutta l'attenzione sul campo da gioco, assicurando un'atmosfera intensa ed eccitante. Lo stadio è destinato a divenire uno dei simboli della città.

Greg Wright Architects
Lion's View | 1999
First Crescent, Camps Bay, Cape Town
Photos: Martin Nicholas Kunz, Michelle Galindo

Dieses 1950 erbaute Haus wurde durch eine zweite Etage erweitert, um Platz für eine in sich abgeschlossene Suite zu schaffen. Die Eingangstür des Hauses, zu der man über eine Brücke gelangt, die über einen Koiteich führt, ziert ein sandgestrahltes, abstraktes Koimotiv. Im fließend gestalteten Innenbereich grenzen Niveauunterschiede der Böden die offiziellen Loungebereiche ab. Überdimensionale Schiebetüren an der Nordwand verbinden den Innenbereich mit dem Pool und dem Außenbereich. Ein offenes Dach im oberen Bereich rahmt die 12 Apostel ein und schafft natürliches Licht.

Adding a second floor to this 1950s house provided space for a self contained suite. The entrance door, reached via a bridge over a Koi pond, is finished in a sandblasted abstract Koi motif. The fluid indoor living space relies on changes in level to define formal lounge areas. Over-sized sliding doors in the north face integrate the interior with the pool and outside living space. An open roof in the upper level frames the Twelve Apostles and provides natural light.

La segunda planta añadida a esta vivienda proporcionó el espacio para un apartamento independiente. La puerta de entrada, a la que se llega al pasar un puente, tiene un motivo koi en chorro de arena. Los espacios interiores vienen definidos por cambios de nivel. Grandes puertas correderas en la fachada norte integran el interior con la piscina y la zona de estar exterior. El tejado descubierto superior ofrece vistas a los Twelve Apostles y luz natural.

L'ajout d'un deuxième étage à la demeure datant des années cinquante a prévu une suite indépendante. La porte d'entrée accessible par un pont au-dessus de la mare aux carpes, se termine par un motif de carpe abstrait. L'espace de vie intérieur fluide mise sur les changements de niveau pour définir les zones de salon officielles. Des portes coulissantes surdimensionnées sur la façade nord intègrent l'intérieur à la piscine et à l'espace de vie extérieur. À l'étage supérieur, un toit ouvert encadre les douze apôtres et fournit une lumière naturelle.

L'aggiunta di un secondo piano a questa casa degli anni '50 ha creato spazio per una suite auto-contenuta. La porta d'ingresso, raggiunta tramite un ponte che passa sopra allo stagno Koi, è rifinita con un motivo Koi. L'ambiente abitativo interno è fluido e si fonda sui cambiamenti di livello per definire le aree di soggiorno formali. Delle porte scorrevoli sovradimensionate sulla facciata nord integrano l'interno con la piscina e l'ambiente abitativo esterno. Un tetto aperto sul livello superiore incornicia i Dodici Apostoli e fornisce una luce naturale.

ID Living
Jardin D'ébène I 2004
Warren Street, Tamboerskloof, Cape Town
Photos: Martin Nicholas Kunz, Michelle Galindo

Dieses auf einem alten Gehöft im Kaphollandstil errichtete Boutique Gästehaus wurde akribisch renoviert und entsprechend einem raffinierten, trendigen, afrikanischen Thema dekoriert. Die eleganten, mit Bad und WC ausgestatteten Räume, wurden in einem modernen Stil dekoriert, der dennoch Erinnerungen an das koloniale Afrika weckt. Ein zum Relaxen einladendes Ruhebett unter subtropischen Bäumen fügt sich harmonisch in den ruhig gelegenen Garten ein, und ein Sonnendeck mit Tauchpool bietet atemberaubende Aussichten auf den Lions Head.

This boutique guesthouse, established in an old Cape Dutch homestead, was meticulously refurbished and decorated in a refined, contemporary African theme. The elegant rooms and their uniquely designed en-suites are decorated in a style that is modern, yet reminiscent of colonial Africa. A relaxing day-bed nestles under sub-tropical trees in the tranquil garden, and a sundeck with plunge pool offers breathtaking views of Lions Head.

Esta exquisita casa de huéspedes, ubicada en una antigua hacienda holandesa, se redecoró de forma meticulosa y refinada con un carácter africano contemporáneo. Las elegantes habitaciones y sus dependencias interiores son de un estilo moderno al tiempo que colonial. Los relajantes sofás-cama bajo los árboles subtropicales en el plácido jardín y el solárium con piscina ofrecen unas majestuosas vistas a Lions Head.

Ce complexe de chambres d'hôtes établies dans une vieille propriété hollandaise du Cap, a été remis à neuf méticuleusement et décoré selon un thème africain contemporain raffiné. Les pièces élégantes et les en suites, conçues de manière unique, sont décorées dans un style moderne qui est encore une réminiscence de l'Afrique coloniale. Des chaises longues pour se relaxer, enfouies sous des arbres tropicaux dans le jardin paisible et un sundeck avec piscine privée offrent des vues panoramiques à vous couper le souffle sur Lions Head.

Questa pensione boutique, costruita in un'antica casa colonica di Cape Dutch, è stata meticolosamente messa a nuovo e decorata con una fine trama contemporanea dell'Africa. Le camere eleganti e le loro suite progettate in modo unico sono decorate in uno stile che è moderno ma al contempo una reminescenza dell'Africa coloniale. Un lettino rilassante si annida sotto gli alberi sub-tropicali nel giardino tranquillo e un ponte scoperto con una piscina per i tuffi offre una vista mozzafiato del Lions Head.

BAINS

Special
Sundowner
White Wine:
Zonnebloem 2003
Chardonnay
Red Wine:
K Johann Rossouw
Blend Quartus
2002
Per Glass
R25
include

Louis Karol
Cape Sun | built 1983, renovated 2006
Strand Street, City Bowl, Cape Town
Photos: Gavin Dingle, Mike Wesson (exterior)

Ursprünglich 1983 für den internationalen Hotelmagnaten Sol Kerzner erbaut, der wegen seiner herausragenden Projekte auch als „Sun King Sol" bekannt ist, wurde die hoch aufgeschossene Silhouette des Gebäudes sofort zu einem Wahrzeichen des Stadtzentrums. Sechs dramatische, gläserne Aufzugsschächte sind schon von weitem sichtbar, und die glamourösen Interieurs erinnern an Szenen aus einer abendlichen Seifenoper im Fernsehen. Das Gebäude wurde großzügig im 45 Gradwinkel zur Straßenführung hin ausgerichtet, um die Aussichten zu maximieren.

Originally built in 1983 for the international hotel magnate, Sol Kerzner, known for his outrageous projects as "Sun King Sol", its tall silhouette became an instant landmark in the city centre. Six dramatic glass elevator shafts are visible from far and the glamorous interiors are reminiscent of an evening soap-opera. The building was deliberately orientated at 45-degrees to the city grid to maximize views.

El magnate de la hostelería Sol Kerzner, famoso por sus escandalosos proyectos como el "Sun King Sol", lo erigió en 1983. Su silueta se convirtió rápidamente en uno de los símbolos de la ciudad. Los seis espectaculares huecos acristalados de ascensor se divisan desde la distancia y el glamuroso interior recuerda al de una telenovela. Su orientación a 45º respecto a la cuadrícula de la ciudad fue intencionada con el fin de optimizar las vistas.

Construite de manière originale, le magnat de l'hôtel international, Sol Kerzner, connu pour ses projets exorbitants comme « Sun King Sol », sa grande silhouette étant devenue un point de repère dans le centre ville. Six gaines d'ascenseur en verre dramatiques sont visibles de loin et les intérieurs glamoureux sont une réminiscence des feuilletions quotidiens du soir. Le bâtiment a été délibérément orienté à 45 degrés de la grille de ville pour maximiser les panoramas.

Costruito originariamente nel 1983 per il magnate degli hotel, Sol Kerzner, conosciuto per i suoi enormi progetti come il „Sun King Sol", la sua elevata silhouette è diventata l'istantaneo simbolo del centro della città. Sei sensazionali vani dell'ascensore, fatti di vetro, si possono vedere da lontano e gli affascinanti interni sono reminiscenti di una soap opera serale. L'edificio è stato orientato deliberatamente a 45 gradi verso la griglia cittadina per massimizzare il panorama.

Southern Sun

LE BAR

Louis Karol
Mutual Heights | built 1939, renovated 2005
Darling Street, City Bowl, Cape Town
Photos: Gavin Dingle, David Southwood (tunnel)

Der im Art Deko Stil entworfene Bürokomplex des Mutual Building, das die Grand Parade Kapstadts überblickt, wurde zuletzt in den Neunzigern genutzt. Seine Verwandlung in luxuriöse Appartements symbolisiert eine Renaissance in der Städteplanung, die junge Talente zurück in die Innenstadt lockt. Die höchsten Etagen wurden miteinander verbunden, um ein über den gesamten Turm reichendes Penthouse zu bilden – mit einer 15 Meter hohen, kirchenartigen Lounge, die durch ihre ikonische Fassade das Gefühl von Raum und Höhe vermittelt.

Mutual Building's art deco office block, which overlooks Cape Town's Grand Parade, was last used in the 1990s. Its transformation into luxury apartments symbolizes a renaissance in urban development that is attracting young talent back to the inner city. The uppermost floors were combined to form a penthouse across the entire turret, with a 15m-high cathedral-like lounge that conveys the sense of space and height promised by its iconic facade.

El edificio de oficinas de la empresa Mutual en estilo art déco con vistas al Gran Parade de Ciudad del Cabo dejó de usarse en la década de los 90. Su transformación en viviendas de lujo simboliza el renacimiento urbano que atrae a los jóvenes valores al centro de la ciudad. Las plantas más altas en la torreta conforman un apartamento con una sala de 15 m de altura que transmite la sensación de espacio y altitud que augura la legendaria fachada.

Le bloc de bureaux art déco de Mutual Building, qui surplombe le Grand Parade de la ville du Cap, a été utilisé dans les années quatre-vingt-dix. Sa transformation en appartements de luxe symbolise la renaissance du développement urbain qui attire les jeunes talents à revenir dans le centre ville. Les planchers supérieurs ont été combinés pour créer un appartement terrasse à travers toute la tourelle, avec un salon de 15 mètres de haut, en forme de cathédrale, qui procure la sensation de l'espace et de la hauteur promise par la façade iconique.

L'art d'eco del palazzo di uffici Mutual Building, che domina la Grand Parade di Cape Town, è stato usato per l'ultima volta negli anni '90. La sua trasformazione in appartamenti di lusso simboleggia un rinascimento dello sviluppo urbano che riattrae i giovani talenti verso l'interno della città. I piani più alti sono stati uniti per formare un attico attraverso l'intera torretta, con una sala d'aspetto alta 15m, simile a una cattedrale, che trasmette un senso di spazio e altezza promesso dalla sua facciata iconica.

SOUTH AFRICAN
SOCIETY

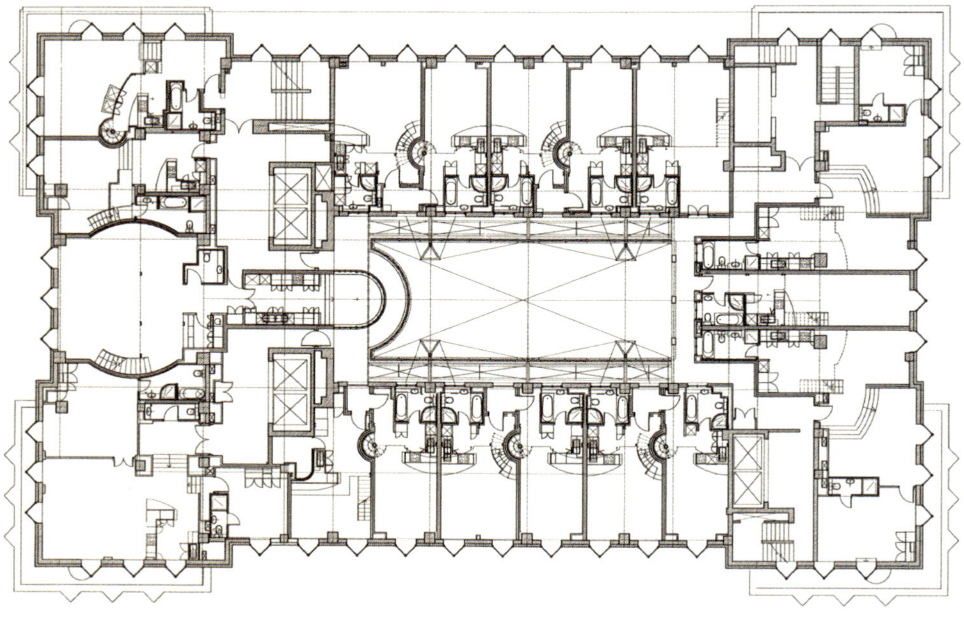

Martin Kruger Associates
BP Centre | 2004
Portswood Ridge, Dock Road, Waterfront, Cape Town
Photos: Mario Todeschini

Dieses Projekt hat einen „Arup Engery Efficient Design Wettbewerb“ für nachhaltiges Design gewonnen. Stark vertiefte Fassaden schützen die Büros vor der Hitze im Sommer, während die Sonne im Winter eindringen kann. Ventilationskamine mit semi-transparenten Reflektorpaneelen sorgen für Belüftung und lassen Licht in das Atrium eintreten, ohne Wärme zu erzeugen. Sonnenkollektoren gliedern die Dachlandschaft, und das Regenwasser wird für Grauwasser-Recycling gesammelt. Die Verwendung der vor Ort erhältlichen Materialien wurde bewusst vorgegeben, um die Kommune mit einzubeziehen.

This project won an Arup energy efficient design competition. Deeply recessed facades protect offices from heat in summer, while allowing solar penetration in winter. Chimney stacks with reflective shelves provide ventilation and allow light to enter the atria without generating heat. Solar panels articulate the roofscape, and rainwater is collected for grey-water recycling. Local materials were specified to enable community involvement.

Este proyecto consiguió un premio Arup al diseño energético. Las fachadas retranqueadas protegen los despachos del calor y dejan pasar la luz en invierno. Los cañones de las chimeneas con tableros reflectantes sirven tanto para la ventilación como para la iluminación del atrio. Los paneles solares modifican la silueta del tejado. El agua de lluvia se recoge para reciclarla. Se seleccionaron materiales autóctonos para implicar a la comunidad.

Ce projet a gagné un concours de design organisé par Arup et portant sur l'efficacité énergétique. Les façades profondément enfoncées protègent les bureaux de la chaleur de l'été tout en permettant la pénétration du soleil en hiver. Les souches de cheminée avec des étagères réflectives fournissent la ventilation et permettent à la lumière de pénétrer dans l'atrium sans régénération de la chaleur. Les panneaux solaires articulent le paysage de toits et l'eau de pluie est ramassée pour le recyclage des eaux usées. Les matériaux locaux permettent d'impliquer la communauté.

Questo progetto ha vinto la gara Arup per progetti validi dal punto di vista energetico. Delle facciate profondamente incassate proteggono gli uffici dal calore dell'estate, permettendo al contempo la penetrazione dei raggi solari in inverno. I camini con dei piani riflettenti forniscono una ventilazione e consentono alla luce di entrare nell'atrio senza generare calore. Dei pannelli solari articolano il paesaggio del tetto e l'acqua piovana viene raccolta per essere riciclata. Sono stati fissati dei materiali locali per permettere un coinvolgimento della comunità.

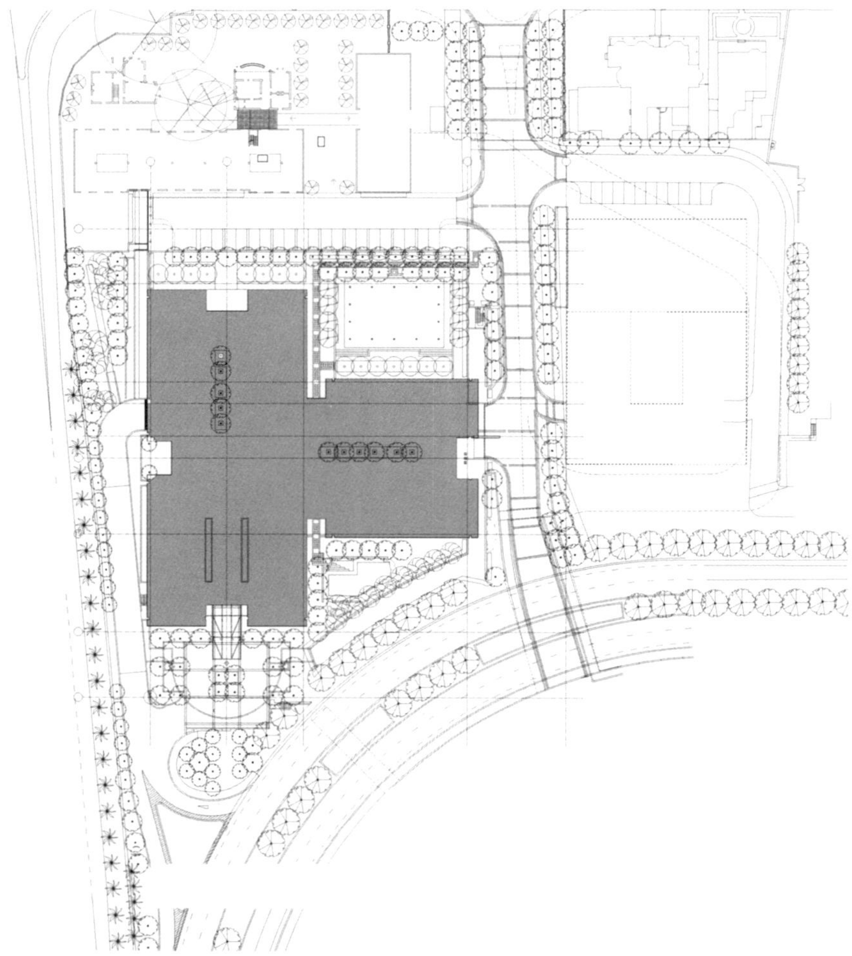

Metropolis Design
Beau Constance | 2004
Constantia Nek, Cape Town
Photos: Wieland Gleich

Dieses auf einem sanierten Weingut errichtete neue Anwesen erhält seine einzigartige architektonische Identität durch die natürlichen Eigenschaften des wunderschönen Weingebietes rund um Constantia. Eine großzügige Küche und der Essbereich bilden das Herz des Hauses, von dem aus verschiedene Räume und Innenhöfe strahlenförmig wegführen. Die Bauweise aus dünnen Betonplatten, innerhalb einer durchlässigen Verkleidung aus Schatten spendenden Lichtblenden, bilden eine Komposition schwebender Elemente, die es dennoch der Landschaft erlauben, weiterhin der dominante Part zu sein.

This new residence, on a redeveloped wine farm, derives its unique architectural identity from the natural qualities of the beautiful Constantia winelands. A double-volume kitchen and dining area form the heart of the house, from which various rooms and courtyards radiate. The construction of thin concrete slabs, within a permeable enclosure of shading screens, forms a composition of floating elements which allows the landscape to remain dominant.

La original identidad arquitectónica de esta casa, rediseñada a partir de una antigua bodega, deriva de la calidad natural de los hermosos viñedos de Constantia. La cocina en dos volúmenes y el comedor forman el núcleo desde el que irradian estancias y patios. La construcción a base de delgados bloques de hormigón rodeados por unos cortinajes traslúcidos da lugar a una composición de elementos flotantes con el paisaje como factor dominante.

Cette nouvelle résidence sur une ferme vinicole relotie, dérive son identité architecturale unique des qualités naturelles des régions vinicoles de la belle Constantia. Une double cuisine et une aire de salon et de salle à manger créent le cœur de la maison, d'où partent différentes pièces et cours intérieures. La construction en fines dalles de béton à l'intérieur d'une clôture d'écrans pare-soleil crée une composition d'éléments flottants qui permet au paysage de rester dominant.

Questa nuova residenza, situata in un'azienda vinicola, deriva la sua identità architettonica unica dalle qualità naturali delle stupende vigne della Constantia. Una cucina doppia e una zona pranzo formano il cuore della casa, dal quale di irradiano diverse stanze e cortili. La costruzione di sottili lastre di cemento, all'interno di una recinzione permeabile di schermi oscuranti, forma una composizione di elementi galleggianti che permettono al paesaggio di rimanere dominante.

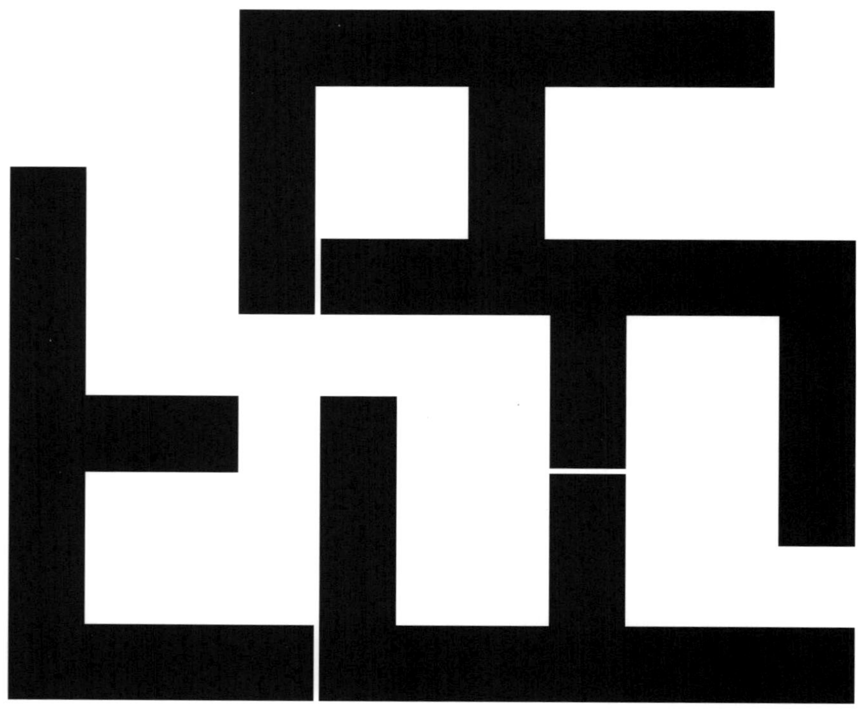

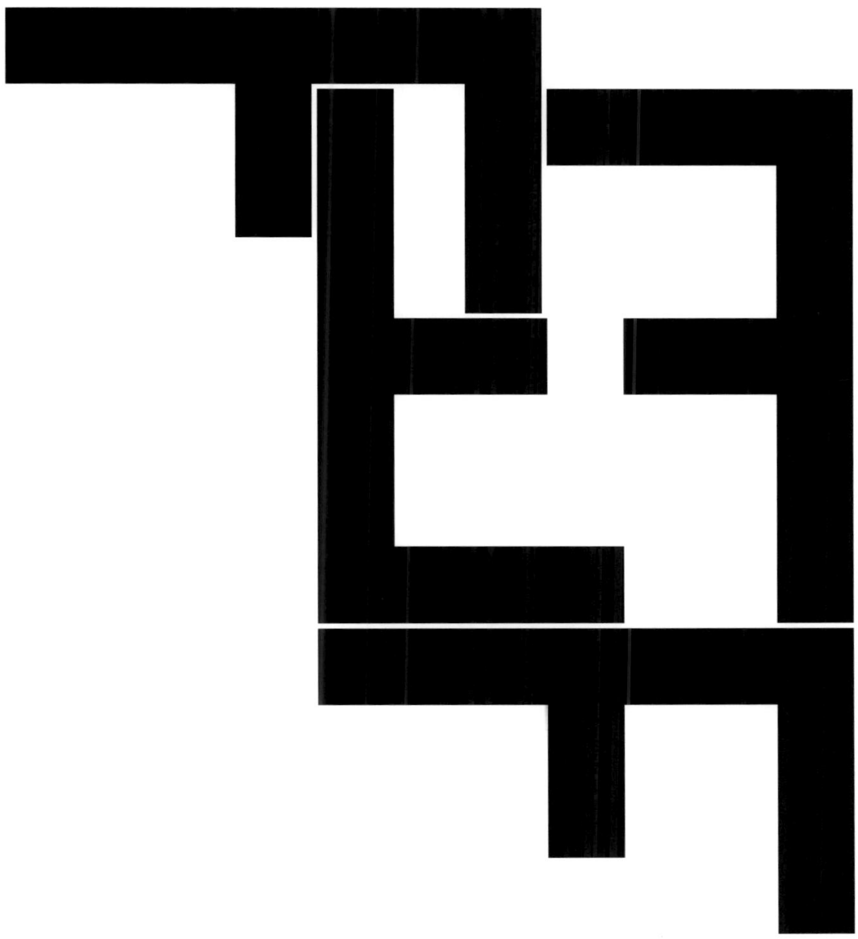

Migo Manz
Focus Contemporary | 2007
Long Street, City Bowl, Cape Town
Photos: Gavin Dingle, Inge Prins

Perfekt gelegen im Herzen der Stadt, erleuchtet diese pulsierende Galerie für zeitgenössische Photographie das Erdgeschoss eines funktionellen Bürokomplexes aus den Sechzigern. Ihre Eckposition garantiert maximale Sichtbarkeit, und die vom Boden bis zur Decke reichende Vollverglasung präsentiert die Werke dem vorbei fließenden Verkehr. Die Ausstellungen finden in der Hauptgalerie statt, während andere Exponate in der 7 Meter hohen Bibliothek zu bewundern sind. Kubische, bewegliche Displays ermöglichen jederzeit eine neue Anordnung, die für jede Ausstellung individuell zugeschnitten werden kann.

Ideally situated in the heart of the city, this vibrant gallery for contemporary photography illuminates the ground floor of a functional 1960s office block. Its corner position maximizes visibility and floor to ceiling glass exposes work to passing traffic. Exhibitions are held in the main gallery while other work remains on show in the 7-meter high library room. Cubic movable displays allow a new arrangement to be tailored for each exhibition.

Situada en el corazón de la ciudad, esta galería de fotografía contemporánea ilumina la planta baja de un bloque de oficinas de los años 60. El hecho de ocupar la esquina maximiza la visibilidad. Los cristales del suelo al techo dejan a la vista las obras. Las exposiciones se organizan en la galería principal. Otras obras permanecen en la biblioteca de 7 m de altura. Los paneles cúbicos móviles permiten organizar el espacio para cada exposición.

En raison de sa situation idéale au cœur de la ville, la galerie vibrante de photographie contemporaine illumine le rez-de-chaussée d'un bloc de bureaux fonctionnel des années soixante. Sa position en coin maximise la visibilité, et le verre du plancher au plafond expose l'œuvre à la modélisation du trafic. Les expositions ont lieu dans la galerie principale, tandis que les autres œuvres restent exposées dans la bibliothèque de 7 mètres de haut. Les affichages cubiques mobiles permettent d'adapter une nouvelle combinaison à chaque exposition.

Situata idealmente nel cuore della città, questa intensa galleria di fotografia contemporanea illumina il piano terra di un funzionale palazzo di uffici degli anni '60. La sua posizione angolare massimizza la visibilità e la vetrata cielo-terra espone i lavori al traffico di passaggio. Le esibizioni sono tenute nella galleria principale, mentre altri lavori rimangono esposti nella libreria alta 7 metri. Dei display cubici movibili permettono di cucire su misura un nuovo allestimento per ogni esibizione.

21.july - 6.sept
talents
focus contemporary photography gallery
talents
focus contemporary photography gallery
21.july - 6.sept
focus contemporary photography gallery

talents
focus contemporary photography gallery
21.july - 6.sept
focus contemporary photography gallery
talents
focus contemporary photography gallery
21.july - 6.sept

Migo Manz
House Llandudno | 2004
Llandudno, Cape Town
Photos: Mark Williams, Jochen Manz (exterior)

Die Hänge von Llandudno mit ihren beneidenswerten Aussichten sind die perfekte Location für dieses ruhige Heim. Oben profitieren vier Schlafräume und ein Großraumbüro vom natürlichen Licht, das durch sich bauschende Vorhänge aus edlem Voile fließt. In dem sagenhaft großen Hauptschlafzimmer genießt man von einer erhöhten Badplattform aus die wunderschönen, ungestörten Ausblicke. Der untere Wohnbereich beherbergt einen Essbereich und eine gemütliche, voluminöse Lounge mit einem Kamin und einem riesigen, eingebauten Sofa.

The slopes of Llandudno, with their enviable vistas, are the location for this tranquil home. Upstairs, four bedrooms and an open-plan office enjoy natural light through billowing voile curtains. In the enormous master bedroom, a raised bath platform allows uninterrupted enjoyment of the magnificent views. The lower living space houses a dining area and an intimate double-volume lounge with a fireplace and giant built-in sofa.

Esta casa tan apacible con unas vistas envidiables se encuentra en las laderas de Llandudno. Cuatro dormitorios y una oficina diáfana ocupan la primera planta; disfrutan de luz natural a través de cortinas traslúcidas. El baño del dormitorio principal, de plataforma elevada, permite seguir disfrutando del panorama. La planta baja cuenta con comedor, un área de descanso con chimenea en dos volúmenes y un gigantesco sofá de obra.

Les collines de Llandudno, avec leurs vues imprenables, sont l'endroit idéal pour cette maison tranquille. À l'étage, quatre chambres à coucher et un bureau ouvert bénéficient de la lumière naturelle passant à travers les rideaux en voile blanc. Dans l'immense chambre à coucher de maître, une plate-forme de salle de bains érigée permet de jouir sans interruption des panoramas magnifiques. L'espace d'habitation inférieur abrite une aire de salon et de salle à manger et un double salon boudoir, avec une cheminée et un sofa géant intégré.

Le pendici del Llandudno, con il loro panorama invidiabile, sono il luogo in cui è posizionata questa tranquilla casa. Al piano di sopra quattro stanze da letto e un ufficio senza pareti divisorie godono della luce naturale che penetra attraverso inondanti tende velate. Nell'enorme camera da letto principale una piattaforma rialzata per il bagno permette di godere ininterrottamente della vista magnifica. La zona soggiorno sottostante ospita un'area da pranzo e una lounge intima doppia con un focolare e un gigantesco sofà incorporato.

Banksy
CAPE TOWN FRINGE DAVID LURIE DOUBLE STOREY BOOKS
IMAGES OF TABLE MOUNTAIN DAVID LURIE BELL - ROBERTS

Peerutin Architects
Beach House | 2008
Clifton, Cape Town
Renderings: Courtesy of Peerutin Architects

Diese luxuriöse Planung überblickt die weltberühmten Clifton Strände Kapstadts. Der Komplex umfasst zwei eingeschossige Einheiten von jeweils 250 m^2 und eine Duplex-Einheit von 400 m^2. Jedes Appartement erstreckt sich über die komplette Breite des Grundstückes und kommt in den Genuss von weitläufigen Aussichten auf den Strand und den Atlantischen Ozean. Das Projekt soll circa April 2008 fertig gestellt sein.

This luxury development overlooks Cape Town's world-famous Clifton beaches. It comprises two simplex units of 250m^2 each, and one duplex of 400m^2. Each apartment extends across the full width of the site and enjoys sweeping views of the beach and Atlantic Ocean. The project is expected to be completed around April 2008.

Esta urbanización de lujo tiene vistas a las célebres playas Clifton de Ciudad del Cabo. Está compuesta por dos unidades de 250 m^2 y un dúplex de 400 m^2. Las tres viviendas ocupan todo el ancho del terreno y disfrutan de unas majestuosas vistas de la playa y del océano Atlántico. La fecha prevista para la conclusión de este proyecto está fijada para abril de 2008.

Ce lotissement luxueux surplombe les plages de Clifton, réputées dans le monde. Il comprend deux unités simplex de 250 m^2 chacune. Chaque appartement s'étend sur toute la largeur du site, jouissant de vues panoramiques sur la plage et l'Océan Atlantique. Ce projet devrait être achevé aux alentours d'avril 2008.

Questo sviluppo lussuoso domina le spiagge di Clifton a Cape Town, famose in tutto il mondo. E' costituito da due unità simplex di 250 mq l'una e da una unità duplex di 400 mq. Ogni appartamento si estende lungo tutta la larghezza del sito e gode della vista immensa della spiaggia e dell'Oceano Atlantico. Si prevede che questo progetto verrà completato intorno ad aprile 2008.

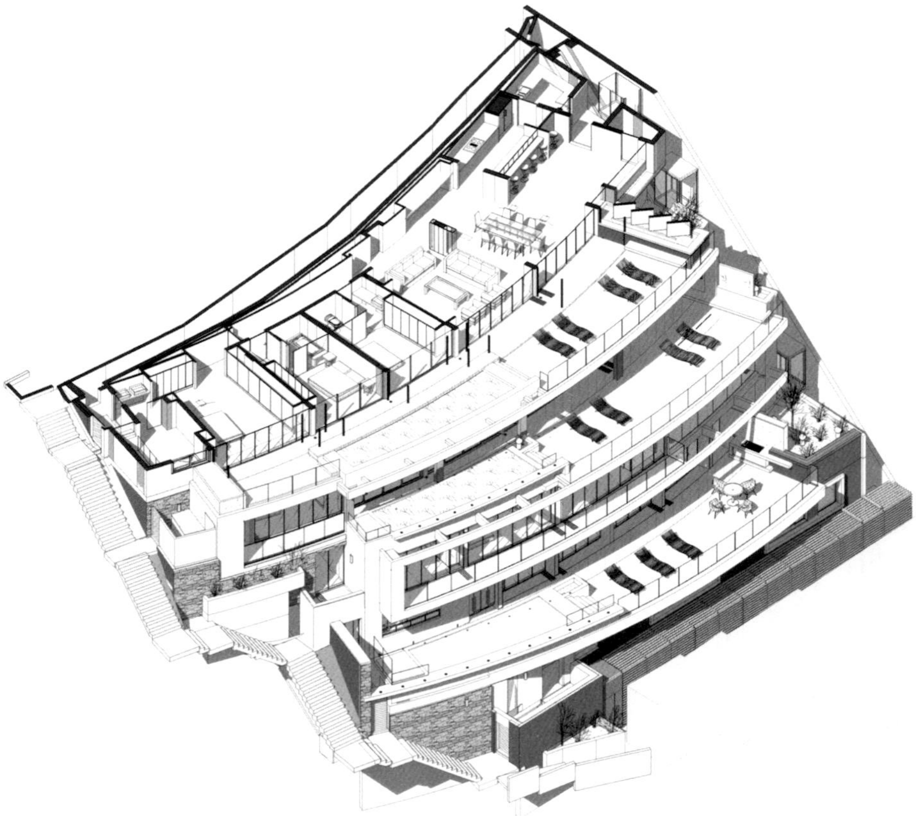

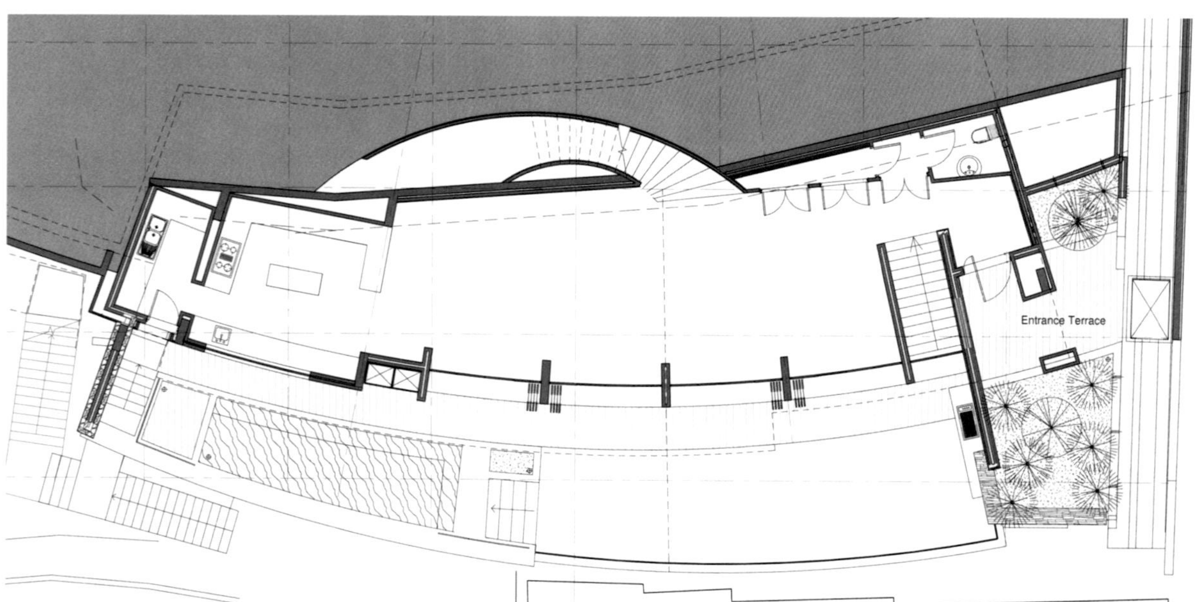
Entrance Terrace

Peerutin Architects
Biddle Cursi | 2004
Camps Bay, Cape Town
Photos: Fiona Barclay Keating

Während Besucher die über einen Koiteich führende Holzbrücke überqueren, werden sie vom Blick auf den Ozean begrüßt, der jenseits einer doppelten Glasfassade sichtbar ist. Eine sich oben befindliche, schwebende Brücke verbindet die zwei Hauptschlafräume miteinander, während Stufen hinunter zum Essbereich führen. Die Raumaufteilung erfolgt eher durch Niveauunterschiede als durch Wände. Die Grenze zwischen Innen- und Außenbereich ist fließend, weil die Pflanzen bis ins Haus hineinwachsen und das selbe Hartholz sowohl für das Pooldeck als auch für den Boden des Essbereiches verwendet wurde.

Crossing the timber bridge over a Koi pond, visitors are greeted by views through a double volume glass facade to the ocean beyond. A floating bridge overhead joins two master bedrooms, and steps lead down to the dining area. Spaces are defined by changes in level, rather than walls. The boundary between inside and outside is blurred by continuing entrance plants into the house, and by using the same pool deck hardwood on the dining room floor.

Al cruzar el puente de madera sobre el estanque de peces koi, el visitante se deleita con las vistas al océano a través de la fachada de cristal de doble volumen. Un puente flotante une los dos dormitorios principales. Al comedor se llega por una escalera. Los espacios se diferencian por cambios de nivel y no por tabiquería. Las plantas que penetran en la casa y la madera de la cubierta de la piscina que continúa en el comedor funden interior con exterior.

En traversant le pont en bois au-dessus de la mare aux carpes, les visiteurs sont accueillis par des panoramas au-delà l'océan, à travers une façade à double verre. Un pont flottant au-dessus relie deux chambres à coucher de maître, et des escaliers mènent à la partie salon et salle à manger. Les espaces sont définis par le changement d'étages plutôt que par les murs. La limite entre l'intérieur et l'extérieur est estompée par l'entrée interminable, construite dans la maison. On a utilisé le même bois de feuillu des bords de la piscine sur le plancher de la salle à manger.

Nell'attraversare il ponte di legno sopra al laghetto Koi, i visitatori vengono accolti dalla vista dell'oceano retrostante una facciata di vetro doppio. Un ponte galleggiante posizionatovi sopra unisce due camere da letto principali e degli scalini portano giù alla zona pranzo. Gli spazi sono definiti dal cambiamento di livello, più che da pareti. Il confine tra interno ed esterno è annebbiato grazie alla continuazione delle piante d'ingresso nella casa e all'utilizzo dello stesso legno duro del pavimento della piscina sul pavimento della sala da pranzo.

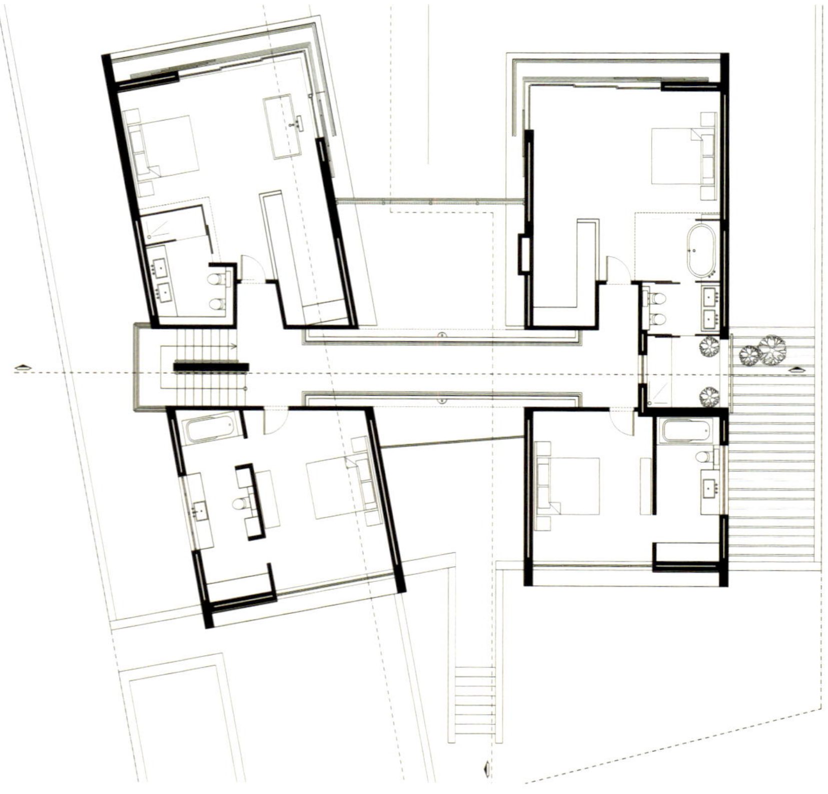

Peerutin Architects
Wembley Square | 2005
Solan Street, Gardens, Cape Town
Photos: Wieland Gleich

Diese Mehrzweck-Sanierung entstand aufgrund einer Privatinitiative und ist eines der ersten Projekte, die im Rahmen des urbanen Neugestaltungsprogramms Kapstadts realisiert wurden. Seine drei Fußgängerzonen bilden eine sichere Umgebung, wo gelebt, gearbeitet und gespielt wird. Der Wohnkomplex umfasst 196 Appartements, während ein kommerzielles Gebäude Büros, Parkplätze und ein Fitnessstudio beherbergt. Diese werden durch eine pulsierende, Indoor-Laufzone miteinander verbunden, wo man Geschäfte, Cafés und Boutique Restaurants findet.

A private initiative, this mixed-use redevelopment represents one of the first projects completed in Cape Town's Urban Regeneration Programme. Its three precincts form a secure environment in which to live, work and play. The residential component includes 196 apartments, while a commercial building houses offices, parking, and a gym. These two are joined by a vibrant indoor street, offering retail stores, coffee shops and boutique restaurants.

Esta reurbanización multiusos de iniciativa privada representa uno de los primeros proyectos del Programa de Regeneración Urbana de Ciudad del Cabo. Sus tres espacios conforman un entorno seguro en el que vivir, trabajar y divertirse. El inmueble residencial cuenta con 196 viviendas y en el edificio de negocios hay oficinas, aparcamiento y un gimnasio. Ambos están unidos por una animada calle interior con tiendas, cafeterías y restaurantes.

Une initiative privée, ce relotissement utilisant le mélange représente l'un des premiers projets achevés dans le programme de renouvellement urbain de la Ville du Cap. Ces trois aires créent un environnement où il y fait bon vivre, travailler et s'amuser. Les composants résidentiels comprennent 196 appartements, ainsi qu'un bâtiment commercial avec des bureaux d'administrations, un parking et un gymnase. Ces deux zones sont reliées par une rue intérieure vibrante, offrant des magasins de détails, des cafés et des restaurants comptoirs.

E' un'iniziativa privata, questo risanamento ad uso promiscuo che rappresenta uno dei primi progetti completati nel Programma di Recupero Urbano di Cape Town. I suoi tre quartieri formano un ambiente sicuro in cui vivere, lavorare e giocare. La parte residenziale include 196 appartamenti, mentre un edificio commerciale ospita degli uffici, un parcheggio e una palestra. Questi due sono collegati tramite una strada esuberante interna, che offre negozi al dettaglio, caffetterie e ristoranti per le boutique.

meme

Wembley Square

WEMBLEY SQUARE

Propfin Design Team
Cape Quarter Extension | 2009
Somerset Road, Green Point, Cape Town
Photos: Richard Wicht

Das Cape Quarter ist ein Lifestyle Einkaufszentrum, das Essen und Einkaufen im Freien in einer sicheren und spannenden Umgebung bietet. Aufgrund seiner enormen Beliebtheit wird es nun bis hin zum angrenzenden Block erweitert. Das Projekt wird Boutiquen der gehobenen Preisklasse anbieten, wobei Ausstattung, Mode, Essen und Unterhaltung fokussiert werden. Die Jarvis Street wird in einen gepflasterten Gehweg verwandelt, wobei die Originalfassaden der bestehenden alten Gebäude erhalten bleiben.

The Cape Quarter is a lifestyle shopping destination that provides an al fresco eating and shopping experience in a secure and exciting environment. Its enormous popularity has prompted an extension in the adjacent block. The project will offer upmarket boutique stores, focusing on décor, fashion, food, and entertainment. Jarvis Street will become a cobbled walkway and the original façades of existing heritage buildings will be maintained.

El Cape Quarter es un centro comercial con mucho estilo donde comer al aire libre y disfrutar con las compras en un ambiente tranquilo y apasionante. Su enorme popularidad ha llevado a ampliarlo, sumándose el edificio adyacente. El proyecto incluye comercios exclusivos de decoración, moda, alimentación y entretenimiento. Se conservarán los edificios protegidos de la calle Jarvis, que se cubrirá con adoquines y se convertirá en zona peatonal.

Style de vie : le Cape Quarter est une destination pour faire du shopping. On y fait des expériences culinaires toutes fraîches et du shopping, dans un environnement sûr et excitant. Son énorme popularité a incité à l'extension du bloc adjacent. Le projet offrira des boutiques concentrées sur le décor, la mode, l'alimentation et les loisirs. Jarvis Street aura une allée pavée et les façades originales des bâtiments du patrimoine existants seront maintenues.

Il Cape Quarter è una meta commerciale da stile di vita che regala un'esperienza di shopping e mangiare all'aperto in un ambiente sicuro ed eccitante. La sua grande popolarità ha provocato l'ampliamento nel blocco adiacente. Il progetto offrirà dei costosi negozi boutique, incentrati su arredamento, moda, alimenti e intrattenimento. Jarvis Street diventerà un sentiero pavimentato e le facciate originali degli edifici esistenti ereditati verranno mantenute.

CAPE QUARTER

Lift / Stairs
Parking Stairs
Andiamo

Andiamo
Andiamo

THE Nose
RESTAURANT
&
WINE BAR
Andiamo

jewellery
jewellery

Revel Fox & Partners
CTICC - Cape Town International Convention Centre | 2003
Convention Square, Foreshore, Cape Town
Photos: CTICC, Gavin Dingle (p 165)

Das in der Nähe der Schnellstraße gelegene CTICC wurde zu einem Katalysator, der das Uferland mit dem restlichen zentralen Geschäftsgebiet verbindet. Das schalldichte, 1500 Sitze umfassende Auditorium, befindet sich an der stärker belebten Seite des Geländes, während die fensterlosen Ausstellungshallen an die Schnellstraßen angrenzen. Restaurants und Ballsäle mit leichtem Zugang zu den Konferenzräumen profitieren von Aussichten auf die Stadt durch die Glasfassade. All diese Elemente werden durch eine dreigeschossige Galerie miteinander verbunden, die sich über die volle Länge des Grundstückes erstreckt.

The CTICC, in its location next to a freeway, has become a catalyst joining the foreshore to the rest of the CBD. The soundproofed 1500-seat auditorium is located at the busier end of the site, while the windowless exhibition halls are situated along the freeway boundary. Restaurants and ballrooms, with easy access to conference facilities, enjoy views of the city through the front glass façade. All of these elements are linked by a three-level gallery that extends the full length of the site.

El CTICC, situado junto a una autopista, sirve de catalizador entre la línea de costa y el centro de negocios de la ciudad. El auditorio insonorizado, de 1.500 plazas, se encuentra al fondo del recinto, mientras que los pabellones de muestras, carentes de ventanas, se alinean junto a la carretera. Restaurantes y salones de baile, con acceso a las instalaciones del centro, tienen vistas a la ciudad a través de la fachada de cristal. Todos estos elementos están unidos por una galería de tres niveles que se extiende a lo largo del edificio.

La CTICC (Conférence internationale de la ville du Cap) est devenue un catalyseur reliant la laisse de mer à la CBD (Convention sur la diversité biologique). La salle de conférences insonorisée, avec 1500 sièges, est localisée au bout du site le plus animé, tandis que les halls d'exposition, sans fenêtres, sont situés le long de la bordure de l'autoroute. Les restaurants et les salles de bals, avec accès facile aux équipements, ont vue sur la façade en verre frontale. Tous ces éléments sont reliés par une galerie à trois étages qui agrandit la longueur totale du site.

Il CTICC, nella sua posizione accanto all'autostrada, è diventato un'unione catalizzatrice tra la spiaggia e il resto della CBD. L'auditorium insonorizzato con 1500 posti è posizionato all'estremità più popolata del posto, mentre le sale esibizioni senza finestre sono situate lungo i confini della superstrada. I ristoranti e le sale da ballo, con un accesso facilitato alle attrezzature per le conferenze, godono della vista della città attraverso una facciata frontale di vetro. Tutti questi elementi sono collegati tramite una galleria a tre livelli che attraversa l'intera lunghezza del sito.

CALTEX

Cape Town International Convention Centre

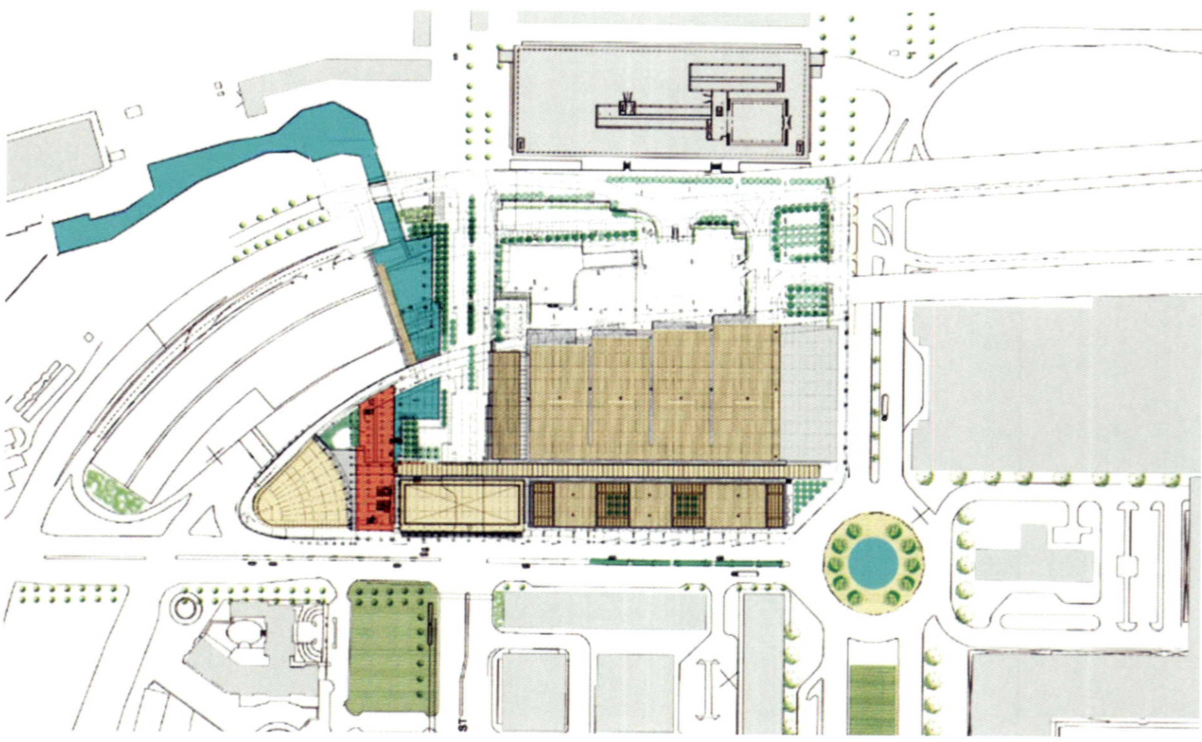

Arabella Sheraton
International Convention Centre

Convention Centre

Reception

← Auditorium 2 1.80
← Meeting Rooms 1.60
← Meeting Suites 1.50
← Meeting Suites 1.70
← Meeting Suites 1.90
1
→ Auditorium 1 1.10
→ Ballroom West 1.21
→ Ballroom East 1.22
→ Meeting Rooms 1.40
→ The Boardroom 1.30
→ The Lounge

Revel Fox & Partners
V&A Marina | 2005
Waterfront, Cape Town
Photos: Lisa Scott, V&A Marina (Pty) Ltd.

Ein still gelegtes Öldepot im historischem Hafenviertel von Kapstadt wurde geflutet und in ein Hafenbecken umfunktioniert, das von Appartements umgeben ist. Es wurde ergänzend zur bestehenden Einkaufs- und Hotelzone entworfen, wobei die Architektur die maritime Tradition des Hafenviertels berücksichtigt. Am Ufer gelegene Gebäude wurden abgestuft, um sie weniger wuchtig wirken zu lassen. Außerdem reduzieren Penthäuser aus leichtem Glas und Stahl den Maßstab der Gebäude. Bewegliche Markisen beleben die Fassaden und schützen vor den Sonnenstrahlen bei gleichzeitiger Maximierung der Aussichten auf das Gebirge und das Meer.

A disused oil tank farm in Cape Town's historic docklands was flooded to form a yacht basin, surrounded by residential apartments. Designed to complement the existing shopping and hotel precincts, the architecture respects the maritime tradition of the waterfront. Buildings at the water's edge have been stepped to reduce their apparent bulk, with light glass and steel penthouses further reducing their scale. Movable awnings enliven the facades and control the sun while maximizing views of both mountain and sea.

Una planta petrolífera en desuso del antiguo puerto de Ciudad del Cabo se sumergió para dar lugar a un puerto deportivo rodeado de viviendas, complemento del centro comercial y del hotel ya existentes. La arquitectura respeta la tradición marinera de la primera línea. Los edificios contiguos al mar se han retranqueado para aligerar su masa aparente y cuentan con áticos de vidrio y acero para reducir la escala. Unas marquesinas móviles controlan la luz solar y maximizan la vista sobre la montaña y el mar.

Une citerne à carburant désaffectée dans les docks historique de la ville du Cap a été inondée afin de créer un bassin pour les yachts, entouré d'appartements résidentiels. Conçue pour compléter les aires de shopping et d'hôtels existantes ; l'architecture respecte la tradition maritime du front de mer. Les bâtiments au bord de la mer ont été construits en étages pour réduire leur volume apparent, ils sont en verre léger et les appartements terrasses en acier continuent à réduire leur échelle. Les tauds mobiles enjolivent les façades et contrôlent le soleil en maximisant à la fois les vues sur la montagne et sur la mer.

Un serbatoio di stoccaggio di olio in disuso presso il molo storico di Cape Town è stato inondato per formare un bacino per gli yacht, circondato da appartamenti residenziali. Progettata per completare i quartieri dei negozi e degli hotel, l'architettura rispecchia la tradizione marittima del lungomare. Gli edifici in riva al mare sono stati fatti a gradini per ridurre la loro evidente massa, con del vetro leggero e degli attici di acciaio che riducono ulteriormente la loro misura. Tende da sole movibili animano le facciate e regolano il sole, mentre massimizzano sia le montagne sia il mare.

Revel Fox & Partners
Vineyard Hotel & Spa | 2006
Newlands, Cape Town
Photos: Pete Maltbie, Courtesy of Vineyard Hotel

Bei der Renovierung dieses Hotels wurden nachträglich hinzugefügte Gestaltungselemente entfernt, wodurch das Original-Kolonialhaus zum Vorschein kam, das 1799 erbaut wurde. Danach wurden unter Berücksichtigung des historischen Kerns zeitgemäße Erweiterungen vorgenommen. Durch die aus Glasschiebeelementen bestehende Straßenfront sieht man einen exquisit gestalteten Garten mit einer fantastischen Gebirgskulisse, durch den ein Fluss hindurchfließt. Der neue, aus Glas und Stahl konstruierte Pavillon, wirkt leicht und transparent und erlaubt es den Gästen, das innen liegende Café, den Pool und die terrassenförmigen Grasflächen als eine ganzheitliche Erfahrung zu genießen.

Renovating this hotel involved stripping away previous additions to reveal the original 1799 colonial home. Contemporary extensions were then designed with respect for the historical core. An exquisitely landscaped garden, with a river flowing through it and mountains beyond, is visible through the frontage of sliding glass screens. The new glass and steel pavilion is light and transparent, allowing guests to enjoy the indoor café, pool and terraced lawns as one holistic experience.

La reforma de este hotel supuso la eliminación de las capas previas para dejar al descubierto la primigenia vivienda colonial de 1799. Las ampliaciones actuales se diseñaron respetando el núcleo histórico. A través de las correderas de cristal del frontal se disfruta de un exquisito jardín paisajista cruzado por un río y con las montañas al fondo. El nuevo anexo de vidrio y acero es liviano y traslúcido, lo que permite disfrutar plenamente del café interior, de la piscina y de las superficies abancaladas de césped.

La rénovation de cet hôtel a décapé les ajouts précédents pour révéler l'habitation coloniale originale de 1799. Les extensions contemporaines ont été conçues alors tout en respectant le fond historique. Un jardin aménagé avec goût, avec une rivière coulant à travers et des montagnes derrière, est visible à travers la façade des panneaux vitrés coulissants. La nouvelle vitre et le pavillon sont légers et transparents, permettant aux clients de profiter du café intérieur, de la piscine et des pelouses sur les terrasses, une expérience holistique.

Il rinnovamento di questo albergo ha implicato la rimozione di aggiunte precedenti per scoprire la casa coloniale originale del 1799. Sono stati poi progettati degli ampliamenti contemporanei rispettando il nucleo storico. Un giardino con paesaggi squisiti, con un fiume che gli scorre attraverso e le montagne sullo sfondo, è visibile attraverso la facciata di schermi scorrevoli di vetro. Il nuovo padiglione di vetro e acciaio è leggero e trasparente, e permette agli ospiti di godere del bar, della piscina e dei prati terrazzati interni come di un'unica esperienza olistica.

Schabort Associates
House Badenhorst | 2006
Welgedacht Estate, Bellville, Cape Town
Photos: Wieland Gleich

Dieses moderne Heim profitiert von seiner Lage inmitten zwei gegensätzlichen Landschaften. Der Wohnbereich mit seinem schwebenden Dach und der Glasflügelfront verschmilzt mit einem offenen Hof, der ungestörte Aussichten auf den Stadtrand bietet. Ein anderer privater Hof, eingebettet zwischen zwei Gebäuden, profitiert von einer Aussichtsplattform über dem angrenzenden Naturschutzgebiet. Bepflanzte Dächer über den Hofanlagen sorgen für eine nahtlose Verschmelzung mit der umgebenden Flora.

This modern home takes advantage of its location between two contrasting landscapes. The living area, with its floating roof and folding glass frontage, merges with an open courtyard that provides uninterrupted views of suburbia. Another private courtyard, sheltered between two buildings, provides a viewing platform over the neighboring nature reserve. Planted roofs on the courtyard structures ensure seamless integration with the surrounding flora.

Esta moderna vivienda aprovecha su privilegiada ubicación entre dos paisajes antagónicos. La sala se estar, con su techo flotante y el frontal de cristaleras plegables, se funde con un patio abierto que ofrece vistas ilimitadas a la ciudad. Otro patio, esta vez abrigado entre dos edificios, sirve de atalaya para divisar la reserva natural aledaña. El tejado ajardinado de la estructura del patio garantiza una perfecta integración con la flora del lugar.

Cette habitation moderne tire profit de son emplacement entre deux paysages contrastants. L'aire de vie, avec son toit flottant et sa façade pliante en verre ; se confond avec une cour ouverte offrant des vues panoramiques sur la banlieue. Une autre cour privée, abritée entre deux bâtiments, est pourvue d'une plate-forme panoramique sur la réserve naturelle environnante. Les toits plantés sur les structures de la cour s'intègrent parfaitement à la flore environnante.

Questa abitazione moderna prende vantaggio dal luogo in cui è situata, tra due paesaggi contrastanti. L'ambiente abitativo, con il suo tetto fluttuante e la facciata di vetrate a soffietto, si fonde con un cortile aperto che fornisce una visuale ininterrotta sui sobborghi. Un altro cortile privato, protetto tra due edifici, fornisce una piattaforma panoramica con vista sulla riserva naturale adiacente. Dei tetti con piante sulle strutture del cortile assicurano l'integrazione continua con la flora circostante.

Stefan Antoni Olmesdahl Truen Architects
Marina 11 | 2004
Bantry Bay, Cape Town
Photos: Stefan Antoni

Dieses natürlich strukturierte Heim zeigt nahtlose Übergänge zwischen Innen- und Außenbereichen. Der Wohnbereich erstreckt sich durch Glasschiebetüren bis zur Terrasse mit einem Pool mit Überlaufrinnensytem und Panoramablick auf den Atlantischen Ozean. Ein mit Travertin veredeltes Treppenhaus, das eine Wendeltreppe ziert, wirkt wie eine zentrale Skulptur in einem überdimensionierten Raum, der den Wohnbereich mit den oberen Etagen verbindet. Die Küche in edlem Kirschholzfinish, kombiniert mit schwarzem Granit, öffnet sich zum Garten, der durch seinen natürlichen Gebirgsbach besticht.

This naturally textured home exhibits seamless transitions between interior and exterior spaces. The living area stretches, through glass sliding doors, onto the deck with a rim flow pool and panoramic views of the Atlantic Ocean. A travertine-clad spiral staircase forms the central sculpture in a triple volume space that links the living area to the upper accommodation levels. The kitchen, finished in cherry wood and black granite, opens onto the garden with its natural mountain stream.

Esta vivienda de texturas naturales presenta transiciones perfectas entre los espacios interiores y exteriores. Las correderas de cristal prolongan la sala de estar hasta la piscina de rebosadero, con vistas al océano Atlántico. Una escalera de caracol recubierta con travertino constituye el elemento central del espacio que comunica la zona de estar con los cuartos superiores. La cocina, en cerezo y granito negro, se abre al jardín con un riachuelo natural.

Cette habitation naturellement texturée montre des transitions entre les espaces intérieurs et extérieurs. L'aire de vie s'étire à travers des portes coulissantes en verre jusqu'à la plate-forme avec une piscine à débordement et des vues panoramiques sur l'Océan Atlantique. Un escalier en spirale revêtu de travertin crée la sculpture centrale, dans un triple espace, qui relie l'aire de vie aux étages supérieurs de l'habitation. La cuisine, en bois de cerisier fini et en granit noir ouvre sur le jardin avec son torrent naturel.

Questa abitazione a trama naturale mostra delle transizioni continue tra gli ambienti interni ed esterni. L'ambiente abitativo si estende attraverso delle porte a vetro scorrevoli, sulla terrazza con una piscina a filo d'acqua e una vista panoramica dell'Oceano Atlantico. Una scala a spirale rivestita di travertino forma la scultura centrale di un ambiente triplo che unisce l'area soggiorno con i livelli di alloggio superiori. La cucina, rifinita con ciliegio e granito nero, si apre sul giardino con il suo torrente naturale di montagna.

11

Stefan Antoni Olmesdahl Truen Architects
St Leon | 2005
Bantry Bay, Cape Town
Photos: Stefan Antoni

Ein über eine Wasserlandschaft führender Plattenweg führt den Besucher zur verglasten, voluminösen Eingangshalle. Oben gelangt man zu einer Brücke über einem skulpturartigen Treppenhaus, das die drei mit Bädern ausgestatteten Schlafzimmer verbindet. Der erste Stock beherbergt eine Küche, Esszimmer und zwei Lounges mit Terrassen, wodurch sich die Grenzen zwischen Innen- und Außenbereich verwischen. Darunter öffnen sich der Unterhaltungsbereich und die Cocktailbar im Erdgeschoss zu einem Holzdeck, das auf zwei Seiten von einem riesigen Endlospool umgeben ist.

Stepping stones over a water feature lead one to the glazed double-volume entrance hall. Overhead, a bridge joining the three en-suite bedrooms of the second floor is reached by a sculptural staircase. The first floor houses a kitchen, dining room, and two lounges with outdoor terraces to blur the boundaries between interior and exterior space. Below this, the ground level entertainment room and cocktail bar open onto a timber deck, surrounded on two sides by a large infinity pool.

Unas pasaderas conducen al vestíbulo acristalado en dos volúmenes. Por encima queda el puente que comunica los tres dormitorios con anexos de la segunda planta. A este se llega a través de una escultórica escalera. En la primera planta se hallan la cocina, el comedor y dos áreas de descanso con terraza que funden el espacio interior con el exterior. Por debajo, la estancia para el esparcimiento y un bar que se abre a un solado de madera, rodeado a ambos lados por una piscina sin límites.

Des tremplins au-dessus d'un dispositif de jet d'eau mène au double hall d'entrée vitré. On accède au pont suspendu, reliant les trois chambres à coucher du deuxième étage, par l'escalier sculpté. Le premier étage abrite une cuisine, une salle à manger et deux salons avec des terrasses extérieures pour estomper les limites entre l'espace intérieur et l'espace extérieur. Au-dessous, la salle de loisirs au rez-de-chaussée et le bar à cocktail ouvrent sur une plate-forme en bois, entourée des deux côtés par une large piscine panoramique.

Dei gradini in pietra sopra a una forma d'acqua conducono alla sala d'ingresso doppia invetriata. Di sopra, il ponte che congiunge le tre camere da letto en suite del secondo piano viene raggiunto dalla scala scultorea. Il primo piano ospita una cucina, la sala da pranzo e due soggiorni con terrazze esterne che offuscano i confini tra lo spazio interno e quello esterno. Sotto tutto questo, la sala intrattenimento e il cocktail bar al piano terra si spalancano verso un pavimento in legno, circondato su due lati da una ampia piscina all'infinito.

Stefan Antoni Olmesdahl Truen Architects

Tamkar | 1999

Camps Bay, Cape Town

Photos: Stefan Antoni

Sinnliche Bögen imitieren die Meeresbewegung und kontrastieren mit den klaren, lateralen Linien in diesem Heim. Beim Eintreten in den untern Bereich, überqueren Besucher einen Koiteich, der sich unter einem dramatischen Treppenhaus befindet, das sich durch das voluminöse Atrium nach oben windet. Ein tiefer liegendes Wohnzimmer aus Travertin bildet das Zentrum dieser Ebene. Durch Glastrennwände, die den Fernsehraum, die Küche und das Esszimmer abgrenzen, fließen die Wohnräume sanft ineinander über. Die oben gelegenen Schlafzimmer und mit Marmor gefliesten Bäder erreicht man über einen zylindrischen Stahlaufzug.

Sensual curves mimic the sea's motion and contrast with clean lateral lines in this home. Entering on the lower level, visitors cross a Koi pond beneath a dramatic staircase that swirls up through the double-volume atrium. A sunken travertine living room forms the focus of this level. Living areas flow into one another, with glass screens defining the TV room, kitchen, and dining room. The upstairs bedrooms and marble-clad en suites may be reached via a cylindrical stainless-steel elevator.

Unas curvas de lo más sensual simulan el vaivén del mar, contrastando con los laterales de líneas puras de esta vivienda. El vestíbulo cuenta con un estanque bajo una espectacular escalera que asciende por el atrio de dos volúmenes. La sala de estar en travertino es el núcleo de esta planta. El paso entre el área de televisión, la cocina y el comedor es fluido gracias a los vanos acristalados. A los dormitorios superiores, con anexos recubiertos de mármol, se llega por medio de un ascensor cilíndrico en acero inoxidable.

Des courbes sensuelles imitent le mouvement des vagues et contrastent avec les lignes latérales impeccables dans cette habitation. En entrant à l'étage inférieur, les visiteurs traversent la mare aux carpes sous un escalier spectaculaire en colimaçon en passant à travers le double atrium. Une salle de séjour en travertin creux crée le centre de cet étage. Les aires de vie coulent l'une dans l'autre avec des vitres en verre définissant la salle de télévision, la cuisine et la salle à manger. Les chambres à coucher à l'étage et les suites revêtues de marbre sont accessibles via un ascenseur en acier inoxydable cylindrique.

Delle curve sensuali simulano il movimento del mare e contrastano con le linee laterali nette di questa casa. Nell'entrare al livello inferiore i visitatori attraversano uno stagno Koi sotto a una scala sensazionale che si snoda attraverso l'atrio doppio. Un salone sprofondato in travertino costituisce il punto focale di questo piano. Le zone abitative confluiscono le une nelle altre, con delle schermate di vetro che definiscono la sala TV, la cucina e la sala da pranzo. Le camere da letto e le suite rivestite di marmo al piano superiore possono essere raggiunte tramite un ascensore cilindrico di acciaio inossidabile.

Thinkspace, dhk
Tobago's Restaurant | 2005
Radisson Hotel, Granger Bay, Cape Town
Photos: Tredeaux Grobler

Das Radisson Hotel befindet sich an einem der malerischsten Küstenstriche Kapstadts. Es grenzt an die berühmte und beliebte Victoria & Alfred Waterfront mit Ausblick auf das Wasser bis zu Robben Island. Die Renovierung des Restaurantbereichs berücksichtigt den stark maritimen Einfluss sowie die Farbpaletten der Grundstückslage. Abends schafft eine Glaswand mit Tiefenätzung einen verführerischen Hintergrund, der ein guter Ersatz für den zu dieser Tageszeit nicht mehr vorhandenen Glanz des Tageslichts ist.

The Radisson Hotel is set on one of Cape Town's most picturesque stretches of coastline. It borders the well known and loved Victoria & Alfred Waterfront, with views across the water to Robben Island. The renovation of its restaurant area respects its strong maritime presence and the color pallet echoes that of the site's location. At night, a deep-etched glass feature wall creates an alluring backdrop to compensate for the absence of daylight splendor.

El hotel Radisson está situado en una de las zonas más pintorescas de la costa de Ciudad del Cabo. Bordea los célebres muelles de Victoria & Albert, con vistas a la isla Robben. La renovación del restaurante respeta la marcada impronta del mar y la gama cromática refleja los colores de su entorno. De noche, una pared acristalada con grabados constituye un fascinante telón de fondo que compensa la falta del esplendor que proporciona la luz diurna.

L'hôtel Radisson est situé sur l'un des extensions les plus pittoresques de la côte. Il borde le Victoria & Waterfront bien connu et aimé, avec une vue donnant jusque sur Robben Island à travers la mer. La rénovation de l'aire du restaurant a respecté sa présence fortement maritime et les gammes de couleurs répercutent l'impact de ce site. La nuit, un mur en verre profondément gravé crée un arrière-plan attirant, compensant l'absence de splendeur du jour.

Il Radisson Hotel è posizionato su una delle distese della costa di Cape Town più pittoresche. Confina con il conosciuto e amato lungomare Victoria & Alfred, con vista, attraverso l'acqua, sulla Robben Island. Il rinnovamento della sua area ristorante rispetta la sua presenza marittima di lunga data e la gamma di colori riflette quella del luogo in cui è situato. La notte, la parete a vetro inciso crea uno sfondo attraente per compensare l'assenza dello splendore della luce del giorno.

Thinkspace, dhk
Riboville Restaurant | 2006
Adderley Street, City Bowl, Cape Town
Photos: Tom Karpinski, Jac de Villiers

Dieser geschützt gelegene Bau war Südafrikas erstes Gebäude, das einen Archtitekturpreis erhalten hat. Die Renovierung seiner Erdgeschoss- und Kellerflächen, die einen gebührenden Respekt verdient, wurde mithilfe der Beratung eines Experten für Kulturerbe durchgeführt. Im Kellerbereich verwandelte man die ursprünglichen Bankgewölbe in einen Weinkeller und einen Essbereich. Das Erdgeschoss wurde restauriert und renoviert, um zwei offene Küchen und Essbereiche zu beherbergen. Zeitgemäße Hinzufügungen zu den aus der Kolonialzeit stammenden Innenausbauten wurden mit größter Sorgfalt durchgeführt.

This protected site was South Africa's first building to receive an architectural award. Deserving respect, the renovation of its ground and basements floors was done with the advice of a heritage consultant. At basement level, the original bank vaults were transformed into a wine cellar and dining area. The ground floor was restored and renovated to house two exposed kitchens and dining areas. Contemporary additions to the colonial finishes were done with great care.

Este edificio protegido fue el primero en Sudáfrica en conseguir un galardón en arquitectura. Las reformas de la planta baja y el sótano se realizaron bajo la supervisión de un asesor de patrimonio. Las primigenias bóvedas del sótano se transformaron en una bodega y un salón comedor. La restauración de la planta baja incluyó dos cocinas abiertas y comedores. La integración de los añadidos modernos al acabado colonial se hizo con mucho esmero.

Ce site protégé a été le premier bâtiment à recevoir un prix architectural. Méritant le respect, la rénovation de ses fondations et de ses sous-sols a été faite avec le conseil d'un consultant de patrimoine. Au sous-sol, les voûtes originales, en rangées, ont été transformées en cellier à vin et en aire de salle à manger. Le rez-de-chaussée a été restauré et rénové pour abriter deux cuisines exposées et des aires de salle à manger. Les ajouts contemporains aux finitions coloniales ont été faits avec le plus grand soin.

Questo luogo protetto è stato il primo edificio del Sud Africa a essere insignito di un premio architettonico. Nel meritarsi rispetto, il rinnovamento dei suoi piani terra e seminterrato è stato eseguito con il supporto di un consulente del patrimonio. A livello del seminterrato le volte originali sono state trasformate in una cantina per il vino e in una zona pranzo. Il piano terra è stato restaurato e rinnovato per ospitare due cucine esposte e due zone pranzo. Le aggiunte contemporanee alle rifiniture coloniali sono state eseguite con grande attenzione.

BLOEMENDAL
WINE ESTATE / LANDGOED
BOUCHARD FINLAYSON
LANDSKROON

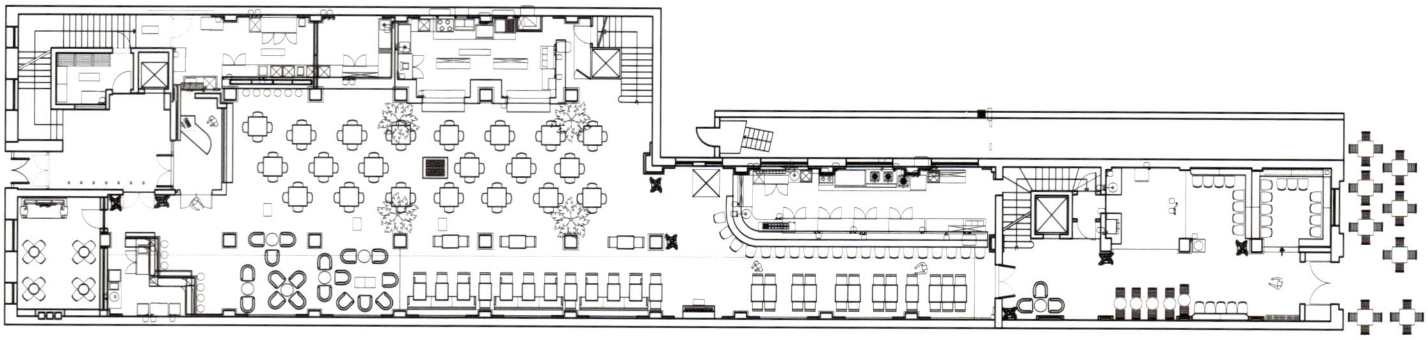

MOËT

Thinkspace, dhk
The Showroom | 2006
Harbour Edge, Greenpoint, Cape Town
Photos: Gavin Dingle

Liebe zum Detail und edle Einrichtungsgegenstände verwandeln diesen minimalistischen, weißen Raum in ein trendiges, dynamisches Restaurant. Da der Platz innen begrenzt ist, schaffen großzügige Spiegelflächen und reflektierendes Glas eine Illusion aus Weite und Licht. Eine großflächige Wand dient gleichzeitig als Weinregal und Kulisse für eine offene Küche, und durch die Fenster der angrenzenden Autoausstellung können edle Luxuskarossen bewundert werden.

Attention to detail and fine furnishings turn this minimalist white room into a contemporary, dynamic restaurant. With limited internal space, tall expanses of mirror and reflective glass create an illusion of volume and light. A large wall of wine forms the backdrop for an exposed kitchen, and luxury cars remain visible through windows to the showroom next door.

El gusto por el detalle y el mobiliario refinado convierten este local en blanco minimalista en un restaurante moderno y dinámico. En el limitado espacio interior, espejos y cristales reflectantes confieren volumen y luz. Un gran botellero en la pared sirve de telón de fondo a la cocina abierta. Los coches de lujo quedan a la vista a través de las ventanas que dan a la exposición.

L'attention aux détails et l'ameublement soigné transforme cette pièce blanche minuscule en un restaurant contemporain dynamique. Son espace interne limité, la grande étendue de ses miroirs et du verre réfléchissant créent une illusion de volume et de lumière. Un large mur de vin crée l'arrière-plan de la cuisine exposée et les voitures de luxe restent visibles à travers les fenêtres donnant sur la prochaine porte de la salle d'exposition.

L'attenzione al dettaglio e un arredamento elegante trasformano questa stanza bianca minimalista in un ristorante contemporaneo e dinamico. Con uno spazio interno limitato, delle grandi espansioni di specchi e vetri riflettenti creano una illusione di volume e luce. Un'ampia parete di vini compone lo sfondo per la cucina scoperta e delle macchine lussuose sono visibili attraverso le finestre che danno lo showroom della porta accanto.

the showroom

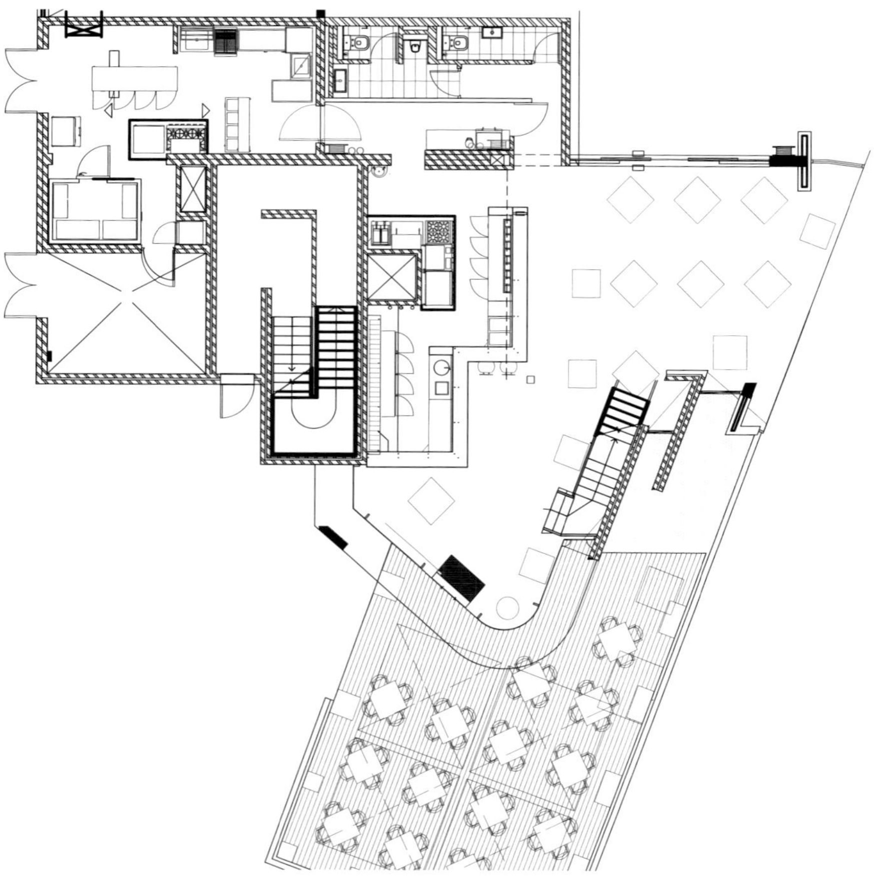

BLOOMSBURY
Investment Cars

CHAMPAGNE
BILLECART-SALMON
CARIMALI

BLOOMSBURY

Victoria & Alfred Waterfront Company
V&A Waterfront | 1992/2007
Waterfront, Cape Town
Photos: Gavin Dingle

Die Verwandlung eines Arbeitshafens in ein spannendes Freizeit- und Erholungsareal begann 1990. Zwischen Robben Island und Table Mountain gelegen, wurde die Victoria & Alfred Waterfront zum meist besuchten Ort Südafrikas. Während hier heutzutage immer noch kräftig expandiert wird, um Unterhaltungsbereiche, Einkaufszentren und Weltklassehotels anzubieten, hat eine sorgfältige Planung das stolze Erbe des historischen Hafenviertels Kapstadts erhalten.

The transformation of a working harbor into an exciting leisure and recreational experience began in 1990. Situated between Robben Island and Table Mountain, the Victoria & Alfred Waterfront has become South Africa's most visited destination. While expanding to offer entertainment venues, shopping malls and world-class hotels, careful planning has maintained the proud heritage of Cape Town's historic docklands.

La transformación de un puerto industrial en un apasionante destino recreativo y de ocio comenzó en 1990. Situado entre la isla Robben y el monte Table, los muelles Victoria & Albert se han convertido en el enclave más visitado de Sudáfrica. Su expansión contará con locales con atracciones, centros comerciales y hoteles de primera. Al tiempo, el meticuloso planeamiento ha conservado el patrimonio de la histórica zona portuaria de Ciudad del Cabo.

La transformation d'un port en activité dans un aménagement de loisirs et de repos captivant a commencé en 1990. Situé entre Robben Island et la Montagne de la Table, le Victoria & Alfred Waterfront est devenu la destination la plus visitée d'Afrique du Sud. En développant des lieux de divertissement, des galeries marchandes et des hôtels de première classe, la planification soigneuse a conservé le patrimoine fier de docks de la ville du Cap.

La trasformazione di un porto in un'accattivante destinazione turistica e di divertimenti iniziò nel 1990. Situato tra Robben Island e Table Mountain, il lungomare Victoria & Alfred è diventato la destinazione del Sud Africa più visitata. Mentre si è espansa per offrire luoghi di intrattenimento, centri commerciali e alberghi di prima classe, una pianificazione curata ha mantenuto il patrimonio dei porti storici di Cape Town.

TOWER
SHOPPING CENTRE

CAPE GRACE

Albert&Partners, Architecture and Design
71 Loop Street, Cape Town
P +27 (0)21 424 8487
F +27 (0)21 424 8367
www.albertandpartners.com
don@albertandpartners.com

Arthur Quinton Darryl Croome Architects
Metropolis, 29 Chiappini Street, Cape Town
P +27 (0)21 417 4300
F +27 (0)21 417 4301
www.aquacor.co.za
info@aquacor.co.za

dhk
9 Somerset Road, Greenpoint
P +27 (0)21 421 6803
F +27 (0)21 421 0670
www.dhk.co.za
cheryl@dhk.co.za

Gabriel Fagan Architects
156 Bree Street, Cape Town
P +27 (0)21 424 2470
F +27 (0)21 424 0749
gabriel@fagan.co.za

GAPP
150 Longmarket Street, Cape Town
P +27 (0)21 424 2390
F +27 (0)21 426 1324
www.gapp.co.za
office@ctn.gapp.net

gmp – von Gerkan, Marg und Partner – Architects
Elbchaussee 139, 22763 Hamburg
P +49 (0)40 88 151 0
F +49 (0)40 88 151 177
www.gmp-architekten.de
Hamburg-E@gmp-architekten.de

Hardenbergstraße 4-5, 10623 Berlin
P +49 (0)30 617 85 500
F +49 (0)30 617 85 601
Berlin@gmp-architekten.de

24 Alfred Street, Cape Town, 8001
P +27 (0)21 425 78 51
F +27 (0)21 425 78 50
gmpcapetown@gmp-architekten.de

Greg Wright Architects
4th Fl, Temple House, c/o Buitenkant & Roeland, Cape Town
P +27 (0)21 465 9775
F +27 (0)21 465 9778
www.gwarchitects.co.za
studio@gwarchitects.co.za

ID Living
28 Vesperdene Road, Greenpoint
P +27 (0)21 439 9296
F +27 (0)21 422 2423
www.idliving.co.za
pascale@idliving.co.za

Louis Karol
2nd Floor, The Palms, 145 Sir Lowry Road, Woodstock
P +27 (0)21 462 4500
F +27 (0)21 462 4550
www.louiskarol.com
info@louiskarol.com

Martin Kruger Associates
153A Kloof Street, Tamboerskloof
P +27 (0)21 424 1113
F +27 (0)21 424 1222
www.martin-kruger.com
uad@martin-kruger.com

Metropolis Design
2A Park Road, Gardens
P +27 (0)21 423 7104
F +27 (0)21 424 7560
www.metropolisdesign.co.za
admin@metropolisdesign.co.za

Migo Manz
2 Long Street, Cape Town
P +27 (0)21 419 8888
F +27 (0)21 419 8888
www.focuscontemporary.co.za
migomanz@aol.com

Peerutin Architects
2nd Floor, Wembley Square North, Solan Street, Gardens
P +27 (0)21 464 4360
F +27 (0)21 464 4399
www.peerutin.co.za
info@peerutin.co.za

Propfin Design Team
13 Hudson Street, Green Point
P +27 (0)21 421 0737
F +27 (0)21 421 0861
www.capequarter.co.za
info@capequarter.co.za

Revel Fox & Partners
117 Waterkant, de Waterkant
P +27 (0)21 425 1710
F +27 (0)21 421 4469
www.revelfox.co.za
design@archifox.co.za

Schabort Associates
The Vineyards, 99 Jip de Jager Road, Bellville
P +27 (0)21 913 0672
F +27 (0)21 913 0619
wynand@sarch.co.za

Stefan Antoni Olmesdahl Truen Architects
109 Hatfield Street, Gardens
P +27 (0)21 468 4400
F +27 (0)21 461 5408
www.saota.com
info@saota.com

Thinkspace, dhk
102 Earlgo Building, c/o Kloof & Park, Gardens
P +27 (0)21 464 4360
F +27 (0)21 464 4399
www.dhkthinkspace.co.za
www.thinkspace.co.za
info@thinkspace.co.za

Victoria & Alfred Waterfront Company
V&A Waterfront Head Office, Portswood Close, Waterfront
P +27 (0)21 408 7600
F +27 (0)21 408 7505
www.waterfront.co.za
info@waterfront.co.za

published and distributed worldwide by
daab gmbh
friesenstr. 50
d - 50670 köln

p +49-221-913 927-0
f +49-221-913 927-20

mail@daab-online.de
www.daab-online.de

publisher ralf daab
rdaab@daab-online.de

creative director feyyaz
mail@feyyaz.com
DAS F-PRINZIP © 2007 feyyaz

© 2007 edited and produced by fusion publishing gmbh stuttgart . los angeles
www.fusion-publishing.com

team
pascale lauber (editor), katharina feuer (editorial assistance, layout)
gavin dingle (editorial assistance, text), alphagriese (translation)

photo credits
coverphoto stefan antoni, backcover gavin dingle
introduction page 7 the graphic ballroom

printed in czech republic
www.graspo.com

isbn 978-3-86654-030-9